T0158987

RIGHT CHOICE

RIGHT CHOICE

EMPOWER STUDENTS TO CREATE THEIR OWN SAFE ENVIRONMENT

JEANETTE BRADLEY M. ED.

RIGHT CHOICE
EMPOWER STUDENTS TO CREATE THEIR
OWN SAFE ENVIRONMENT

Copyright © 2019 Jeanette Bradley M. Ed.

All rights reserved. No part of this book may be used or reproduced by any means, graphic, electronic, or mechanical, including photocopying, recording, taping or by any information storage retrieval system without the written permission of the author except in the case of brief quotations embodied in critical articles and reviews.

iUniverse books may be ordered through booksellers or by contacting:

iUniverse
1663 Liberty Drive
Bloomington, IN 47403
www.iuniverse.com
1-800-Authors (1-800-288-4677)

Because of the dynamic nature of the Internet, any web addresses or links contained in this book may have changed since publication and may no longer be valid. The views expressed in this work are solely those of the author and do not necessarily reflect the views of the publisher, and the publisher hereby disclaims any responsibility for them.

Any people depicted in stock imagery provided by Getty Images are models, and such images are being used for illustrative purposes only. Certain stock imagery © Getty Images.

ISBN: 978-1-5320-6291-9 (sc)
ISBN: 978-1-5320-6292-6 (e)

Print information available on the last page.

iUniverse rev. date: 03/04/2019

CONTENTS

I.

PLAN OF ACTION

I. PLAN OF ACTION

Concepts of discipline will be taught daily.
Discipline routines and procedures will be practiced.
Students will be taught how to understand the concept of choices.
Consequences will be realistic and consistent.

I. PLAN OF ACTION

This Plan of Action section will present the basic concepts of the Right Choice Program.

The suggestions for "how to begin and then carry out the program" are presented in part IV which deals with Right Choice Implementation.

Since one of the basic concepts is that discipline needs to be TAUGHT, the teacher needs to set aside time EACH day to teach the lessons of the Right Choice Program.

The lessons are written as prompts and suggestions to teach the meaning of the concepts.

The teacher can elaborate, or divide the lessons into small sections as needed to best suit the class's needs.

Teachers need to be sure that the students UNDERSTAND the concept being presented and then give them the opportunity to PRACTICE what is being taught.

The first thing the teacher needs to establish is his expectations in his classroom.

It can never be assumed that students know how to act or what to do in every situation.

The teacher needs to explain SPECIFICALLY what to do (STATE FACTS CLEARLY and use a step-by-step method) and how to act in the daily routines of the class.

After the expectations are established, the teacher needs to provide time to actually PRACTICE the expectations. (This practice if often overlooked.)

Examples of things (there are more) to practice are:

Practice putting away materials and supplies.
Practice getting materials and supplies out.
Practice going through the lunch line and sitting at the table.
Practice leaving the lunch room.
Practice speaking SOFTLY and moving quietly around the classroom.
Practice leaving and entering the classroom.
Practice raising your hand and waiting to be called on to speak.
Practice using polite manners, "Please," "Thank you," etc.

Practice here means teaching students EXACTLY how to do something.

EXAMPLE: You tell students to clean out their desk or personal supply storage area.

What happens: Students take it all out and then they PUT IT ALL BACK.

Teach them: They need to be taught WHAT TO PUT BACK and what THEY need to CHOOSE to do with the rest - take it home or throw it away. (If you advise them to throw it away, they "tend" to say, "The teacher MADE me throw away my things." - Even though it was obviously trash.)

It is STRONGLY RECOMMENDED that the teacher stop class and take a few minutes to practice EVERY TIME a rule is forgotten during the FIRST FEW WEEKS of using this program.

This will be in addition to the instructional time dealing with the lessons.

When the students see that you will not let things slip by, they will be more apt to remember the correct procedure.

The class time that is "lost" by the interruption will indeed be "regained" by good conduct for the rest of the year!

The teacher's positive attitude that his/her class CAN AND WILL be well behaved will play a great part in achieving this because students really do measure up to what is expected of them. "My teacher said," still carries weight.

The concept of CHOICES - the students CHOOSE - needs to be stressed DAILY. At first, students need to be reminded CONSTANTLY that THEY ARE CHOOSING. They are CHOOSING THEIR CONSEQUENCES - positive or negative by their actions (what they do or do not do).

For the first three or four weeks all routines, procedures, and social skills need to be practiced and talked about for at least 20 - 30 minutes a day.

This can be spread throughout the day.

Many teachers tend to TELL students to behave, possibly not realizing that students need to be TAUGHT AND THEN GIVEN PRACTICE in discipline.

Some teachers stop teaching discipline as soon as their class seems to settle. Math and reading are taught and practiced all year. Discipline needs the same attention.

The more time that is spent at first TEACHING AND PRACTICING the LESS time will be needed later to CORRECT.

Since this program is focused on empowering students to be responsible for their conduct (their CHOICES), it is essential for them to help decide on the class rules.

Students will feel more responsible for something that they had a part in making.

Keep in mind that it is better to have a few rules that are REALLY kept than it is to have a list that covers "all" and monitoring all of them becomes too burdensome.

The list REALLY needs to be posted. When a rule is broken, it is easy to refer to the list by saying, "Dotty, you broke rule three. We will discuss it later," and continue with class. (Suggestions for rules and discipline charts/cards are presented later in this book.)

If you teach nothing but good discipline SUCCESSFULLY during the first few weeks, you will have a terrific year ahead of you!

CHOICES

Every minute of your life, you chose what you do. Along with those CHOICES comes RESPONSIBILITY and CONSEQUENCES.

This is a concept that students need to be taught.

The student cannot say, "He made me," or "She told me to." Even if the other student tried to influence him, it was still his CHOICE to listen to the other student. Therefore, the positive or negative consequences were CHOSEN by the student doing the act.

The teacher needs to work with students so that they are capable of making RIGHT CHOICES.

Also, the teacher needs to believe that all students can be good; all are able to change, if necessary. Even students who have been "labeled difficult" can CHOOSE to change and be better.

It is essential for the teacher to DISCUSS CHOICES with the student. During the discussion, question such as the following are important!

> How did that make you feel?
> Did you let someone take charge of you?
> Was it a good choice for you? Why? Why not?
> Would your parents be pleased?
> How do you feel about the consequences?
> How did your choices effect others?
> How could you have made a better choice?

MOST IMPORTANT:

> How can I help you make better choices?
> How can you help yourself?
> When will you start?

How will I know you REALLY mean it?
Will you put that in writing?

If the student CHOSE to go to the office by being disruptive, disrespectful, or not following directions:

The student needs to be reminded that he/she CHOSE to be there!

The teacher did not do it. (Students almost ALWAYS want to say that the teacher put them there.)

Students need to be TAUGHT that it was a result of THEIR CHOICES.

Questions in the office should also include:

How do you plan to get the teacher to take you back?

What will you do if she does not?

(We know the teacher will eventually, but it is good for the student to think about the NEED to get back in class.)

I know the teacher LIKES you, but does she/he WANT to have problems?

After the consequence for what happened is completed, the student MUST APOLOGIZE to the teacher and ASK to be taken back. This is usually hard for the student, but remind the student it was his CHOICE to leave the class.

As the students begin to realize that they really are CHOOSING and that they are giving themselves consequences, they begin to make more lasting changes in their behavior.

CONSEQUENCES

Consequences play a key role in maintaining discipline.

Students need to realize that good consequences happen for good conduct. Good consequences include such things as establishing a good reputation, making good grades, having friends, being pleased with yourself, etc.

Consequences for unacceptable behavior need to be tough, fair, and in line with the nature of the deed.

To suspend a student for not putting trash in the proper place would not be fair, because it is too severe for the action.

In considering consequences, the following components should be included.

1. Consequences need to be stated clearly.
2. There should be a series of three or four steps.
   (Not just, "You will be choosing to be out of class.")

EXAMPLE:

First offense -	A warning to the student.
Second offense -	A check mark or color change.
Third offense -	Student and teacher conference about the situation.
Fourth offense -	STUDENT calls parent - teacher monitors call. Call should begin, "I CHOSE..."
Fifth offense -	Student, teacher, parent and principal conference to address the problem.

3. Consequences are given to bring about a change in behavior, not to punish or get even with the student.

4. Both the teacher and the principal MUST be CONSISTENT.
5. Consequences should be for the "offenders" and not the entire class (when only some were disruptive).

CONSISTENCY is hard because:

> Misconduct often occurs when a teacher does not have time to address a situation.

> The class discipline system is too complex, or too harsh, or too vague for the teacher to carry through. So, the teacher avoids the situation until it is intolerable or out of control.

> Teachers forget to AVOID stating consequences that they do not plan to carry out. In frustration, they say such things as: "Everyone will copy twenty (20) pages of the dictionary." This is too much and not at all effective in improving discipline.

> Sometimes, it is easier to ignore the situation than it is to address it.

> Students try (sometimes successfully) to bargain their way out of consequences. "I promise never to do it again if I do not have to call my dad."

> Students know how to wear teachers down or how to get on their nerves. They know when and how far they can "push" the teachers if consistent discipline is not followed.

CONSISTENCY IS ESSENTIAL.

EFFECTIVE CONSEQUENCES

Consequences must be stated so that students understand exactly what is meant.

> First, listen to students. Hear their side! Even if you have to point out their errors.
>
> Conferencing with students.
>
> Not lecture - conferencing to discuss reasons for the problem and plans to do better.

Find out as much about the student from the office folder on the student, or other school personnel as possible to be prepared for the conference.

Time out! A MUST! In an area that the student will feel isolated, but still be visible to the teacher for supervision.

Taking away a privilege.

Detention - Be SURE parents are notified AHEAD OF TIME IF A STUDENT IS DETAINED after dismissal. Detention is MOST effective if it is about two hours of just sitting - no work - that makes the time pass faster.

Call parent (at home or at work).

Remember that it is the parents' responsibility also! A note is acceptable if there is no phone.

It is recommended that the student write the note and tell the parents what he CHOSE to do. The signed note SHOULD be returned within 24 hours for the student to remain in class. The student needs to understand, that the signed note is his TICKET to get to stay in class. Be SURE to check what the note says before it goes home.

It helps to remind the students that they NEVER FORGET to wear shoes to school. They want to remember those. So, when he puts on his shoes the next morning, he should be SURE to remember the note.

If the student DOES return without the signed note, have the principal assist in contacting the parent (and keeping the student).

Have the students write, in great detail, all that happened and how it could have been better. This is also effective for a constant talker. Let the talker write what he wants to say.

In some cases, it helps to limit the number of times a constant talker may be allowed to speak. Let that student keep a "tally" on his desk, as a reminder, if the times he has used and how many he was left.

It makes him/her aware of how often he/she speaks. This gives the student a visual picture of the problem.

In like manner, the teacher can limit how far a student may move from his desk by a piece of tape on the floor that shows the student's space. Or limit how many times a student may be in another area of the room.

The best consequences come from students. Have a conference with those students who have the most difficulty following the rules.

Their suggestions will be effective because they tend to say what they dislike the most. They feel that it will be for others. They usually do not feel that they will be the ones receiving the consequence.

If sentence writing is used - make it difficult but productive.

It is better (and harder) to write 30 - 45 (depending on the grade level) DIFFERENT sentences on how to be better than 100 "I will be good in school." (This type - I will be good. - is NOT recommended.)

If sentences are used as a consequence, the completed work is the ticket back to class.

For students who can not get along it is VERY effective to have them write 30 - 60 NICE things about each other. They may even help each other.

Experience shows that they will either get along better or stay apart and ignore each other. They do not want that assignment again since the number will be doubled. They can not repeat what they used before.

These concepts will be successful only to the degree that the teacher determines they will. Of course, COMMON SENSE and CARING for students play a major role.

Students need TEACHING AND PRACTICE IN DISCIPLINE, but they also NEED THE TEACHER'S CARE, ENCOURAGEMENT, AND SUPPORT.

II.

USE OF A POSITIVE APPROACH

II USE OF A POSITIVE APPROACH

Students need to be aware that the teacher cares for them.

Students need to know that the teacher cares about their feelings and wellbeing.

Students are taught how to give and receive respect.

Students NEED to know they can go to the teacher for help if they have problems with the lessons, with other students, or with other matters. (And not be in trouble for seeking help.)

When necessary, the teacher will seek assistance for the student from the counselor, the nurse, the principal, or assistant principal.

II. USE OF A POSITIVE APPROACH

A positive approach needs to include the following types of action.

Acceptance of every student and of their needs.

Patience with each student's failures and frustrations.

Constant reinforcement of what should be done for the student to be successful as a citizen of the class and of the world.

Praise that addresses the SPECIFIC ACTION of the student.

"Douglas, I like the way you talked to Brad in your reading group." "Marcy, your paper is neater, I'm glad to see you try harder." The specific is more effective than general praise.

Words such as "Super," and "Terrific," said to the class in general, do little to make the student feel pleased with the effort that was put forth.

Specific praise lets the student know what was good about his/her action. It also tells the student the particular effort was successful and should be repeated.

Specific praise needs to be sincere and varied and given to all students - individually.

Praise needs to be used to teach students the success of what they do - NOT to get students to be teacher pleasers.

A positive approach demands that for the good of the class, action be taken immediately to stop disruptive behavior. Avoid making the student defensive. State the facts simply and move on with the lesson.

A positive approach needs to direct students to strive for self-discipline and self-acceptance. The student needs to learn to decide for himself why certain actions are acceptable (for the good of self and others) or why some actions are not good.

Allow the students to get class recognition by encouraging them to respond to such questions as:

Tell us what you like about the way you did that good report.

Explain how you did such a great job on your science paper.

Remember to let the student be heard.

Give each student time to tell his side (of anything). Allow the student the opportunity to express orally or in writing what was wrong with the action in order for the student to see a need for a change.

Be near the student and speak softly when you want to stop any action. (Try to avoid calling across the room.)

The teacher MUST REMAIN CALM! Allow for time out! Time out is COOL DOWN TIME for BOTH student and teacher. Avoid yelling. A loud voice will make the student feel threatened. It can also make the student rebel and try to demand his "rights" - what he feels he needs in a stressful situation.

Above all, treat the student with respect. Do not embarrass the student in front of the class. The student must know you are concerned about how he feels.

A positive approach treats a student as an individual. The student needs to learn that fair does not mean equal. The teacher is fair when she gives the student the attention, assistance, care, and correction that is best for him.

This is a hard concept for students. They often want "fair" for themselves and "justice" for others.

This is not to say that consequences should vary in every instance (to be fair), but the students need to understand that the teacher has the right to "consider the circumstances and each student's needs" in any situation.

BEFORE you have a problem, be SURE that each student is made to FEEL CARED ABOUT AND IMPORTANT in your class! When students feel that you LIKE them, they are more LIKELY to cooperate!

TELL EACH student in a meaningful way, that you are glad to have him. It REALLY makes a difference.

Students learn from what they observe in others. If the teacher is kind, fair, and shows respect for the student, the student will be more likely to follow the example than not.

III.

COMMITMENT
FROM TEACHER

III. COMMITMENT FROM THE TEACHER

The teacher will work to carry out the plan of Right Choice every day.

The teacher will maintain a positive attitude about discipline.

The teacher will remember that change takes teaching, time, and practice.

III YOUR COMMITMENT

Teachers are the key to good discipline.

The way you enter the room "tells" the student who is in charge. Students can "sense" if the teacher cares, if the teacher intends to be in charge, or if the teacher Is a "push over."

Teachers who want a well disciplined class will have one, because they will make their class exciting and a fun place to be.

Teachers who are committed to having good discipline, stop class, if necessary, to gain order, to redirect students, or to prevent a disruption from occurring. They know that time spent to reinforce acceptable behavior is time well invested.

Teachers need to make students realize that education is a PRIVILEGE and that disruptions take away from that privilege.

The teacher's attitude toward students sends out signals to the students. "This will be a great day." Or, "This will be a great year." Students can "read" the teacher better than they read the books. Students also need to be motivated. Motivation is a very challenging area. This book contains suggestions to do so.

Some methods of motivating students are:

Use hands-on activities.

Try cooperative learning. Students are more likely to be involved in the lesson when doing group work. Social skills for group work need to be taught and practiced.

Give students something to work toward or look forward to doing.

EXAMPLES: You may work on your mural as soon as you
             complete your work.
             As soon as you finish this work, we'll make
             plans for the puppet show.

Assessment and drills should not be too lengthy. It is just as easy to assign 10 - 15 problems as 25 - 30. Students dread long assignments.

Active participation in class helps. Doing, not just listening, helps also.

Excitement from the teacher is great, because when the teacher is really excited, the students are also.

Let the students know their work will be displayed.

Let them know that the principal wants to see their work. If you have a really reluctant student, tell him/her to take the completed assignment to the principal. (Arrange this ahead of time with the principal.) If the student knows that at 2 o'clock he will take his assignment to the principal, he will most likely have it ready for praise.

Give work on their level. Students work better when they see that they are being successful. Class assignments - every student ALWAYS doing the exact same assignment - results in some having work that is too easy and some that is too difficult.

Those with work that is too easy can become disruptive.

Those with work that is too difficult can become frustrated.

Some people do not believe that competition is good for children. Our society thrives on competition, especially in all types of sports.

Therefore, our students grow up with the idea of winners and losers. They understand that to win, one must work hard.

Great success can be achieved by having a teacher extend an invitation to another class, to do better in a subject than her class.

The losing team should be taught how to show good sportsmanship by offering friendly praise to the winner.

Losing makes the students work harder to do better. They will be very motivated to achieve better results!

This also works with challenging a class in another school in the district.

Children are never happy with a long assignments. Motivate them to do better by offering the opportunity to do less. "Your math assignment is the 15 problems at the top of page 65.

You may choose to do any 10 of these problems, but you MUST make a grade of 85 or better. If you do not make at least 85, you will need to do the 5 you skipped. They will work harder to do better, and not have to do all 15."

This also works with other subjects. Example: Assign 20 sentences in grammar to find the verbs. They may do only 10, but they MUST make at least 80 or they need to complete the rest of the assignment.

Students LOVE CHOOSING which of the assigned work they will do (ANY problems/ANY sentences).

Homework is given to reinforce the skill being taught, If students can show that they understand the concept by making at least 80 or 85, it is not necessary for them to do "piles" of work.

A FUN activity is highly motivational. An all time favorite is a bubble gum blowing contest!

The teacher provides the gum, and after the contest, the teacher sees that ALL gum is thrown away in something like a plastic bag for disposal.

REASONS FOR MISBEHAVIOR

STUDENTS
  misbehave because:

TEACHERS
  therefore must:

1. They want attention.

1. Give lots of specific praise and attention. Teach acceptable ways to get attention.

2. They want to "cover up" their lack of skills.

2. Treat students with patience, dignity, and respect. Set the student up for success - teach on his ability level.

3. They want power in class.

3. Involve students in class decisions, rules, and routines. Avoid power struggle by refusing to be part of a verbal struggle. State the facts, "You broke rule 3 and will call your parents," and move on with class.

4. They want to get revenge.

4. Be sure the student knows you really care and avoid giving them a reason to think they are not treated right. Be understanding when a bad situation occurs. Above all avoid condemning the child WITH the action! Stay calm.

Remember:

All students can be taught to make Right Choices.
It takes teaching, practice, and patience!

PREVENTIVE MEASURES EFFECTIVE IN MOST SITUATION

Show that you care. TELL EACH student that you are glad he is in your room.

Communicate with the students.
Communicate with the parents.

Remind the students of CHOICES. THEY are making the choices.

Use humor often for laughter (but NEVER AIMED AT THE STUDENT).

Be CONSISTENT! An absolute must for good discipline.

Enforce consequences fairly.
Remember: Fair means to give each student what he needs. If a student CHOOSES to do an unacceptable act, then that student is CHOOSING to get a negative consequence when he is caught.

Consequences are used to bring about a change in behavior. Therefore, consequences should FIT the needs of the student. Students respond differently to various consequences.

Consequences do NOT have to be the same for every student. While it is USUALLY done that way and fine to do so, students need to be aware that it may NOT necessarily be that way. This is hard when they make poor CHOICES. They run the "risk" of a consequence that they may not like.

Allow FREE TIME for a few minutes at the end of each lesson. It is fun to earn it, and it is something that they can lose, depending upon THEIR CHOICES.

Show that you are proud of them.

Take time to show interest in each student.

Be sure to provide FUN and EXCITEMENT. School can be so dull!

Work to stay focused on the NEEDS OF EACH STUDENT. HARD to do.
SMILE! IT WILL MAKE THEM FEEL WELCOME.

PREVENTIVE MEASURES FOR STUDENTS SEEKING ATTENTION

Effective suggestions for preventing problems:

Show interest in every student.

Be mobile. Move around often enough to maintain student attention.

Make eye contact often.

Be consistent! Be consistent! Be consistent!

Prevent lag time. Have something for students to do all the time.

Develop class awareness. The teacher needs to be AWARE of all that is happening in the class - all of the time.

Provide opportunities for socializing. A few minutes of FREE TIME is great for this. Plan what is and is not acceptable conduct during FREE TIME. This is great because they can earn it or lose it. Students REALLY enjoy FREE TIME.

> Suggested acceptable conduct during Free Time: Speak softly. Let others have a turn to speak. If volume gets loud, FREE TIME will end.

Use SPECIFIC words to praise and encourage efforts and success.

> Examples: "B.W., you did an excellent job on your oral report because you used exciting verbs."

> Words such as "Super" and "Terrific" stated in isolation, do little to encourage students.

Make certain that EVERY student receives recognition for effort and encouragement to continue striving for success.

Use light humor. Enjoy your class. Strive to make your class the one that they enjoy the most!

Add a little fun every day. Everyone likes to have a good time.

PREVENTIVE MEASURES FOR STUDENTS HAVING TROUBLE WITH SKILLS

Give appropriate tasks.

Communicate with students - be sure they understand what you are teaching them.

Provide clearly stated criteria for tasks.

Use shorter tasks - higher quality. It is better for students to complete 20 math problems correctly, than complete 35 with most done incorrectly.

Teach problem solving skills:

> Example: What do I want to know?
> What information is available to me?
> How can I use the information to arrive at an answer or conclusion?
> How can I check my answer for accuracy? etc.

TEACH students to listen to directions the FIRST time. INSTRUCTION should be given as often or as much as the student needs, but directions need to be given once.

"How to follow directions" is a skill that MUST be taught. Directions need to be exact and clearly stated. Give very SPECIFIC (step-by-step) directions.

Assign peer workers as needed.

Make tasks FUN AND EXCITING. It will help you also!

Help students be pleased with THEIR best efforts.

Remind them of past successes.

Avoid giving written assignments (in content areas) as consequences. They may feel that the subject matter is a "negative consequence." It is more effective to give 30 or 40 DIFFERENT SENTENCES on "How To Be A Better Student" or "How To Behave Better In Class." It is difficult to think of that many.

Schedule difficult activities first.

Get excited about your lessons. It's contagious.

PREVENTIVE MEASURES FOR STUDENTS WHO SEEK POWER

Show you care about each student.

Use pleasant language and ACT the part of being in control of the class - YOU ARE!

Never argue with the student. State the facts and move on with the lesson.

> Example: "Katyan, you broke rule three. The consequence is a conduct cut."
>
> If Katyan continues to talk, tell her that she is CHOOSING MORE consequences which may include removal from the class.
>
> Do not prolong the confrontation - that is EXACTLY what the student wants.
>
> The student wants you to "TRY TO MAKE HIM/HER" do something.
>
> Simply remind the student that he/she has the CHOICE AND the CONSEQUENCE - good or otherwise.

Remain calm. (Often this is HARD to do.)

Allow the student to have TIME OUT.

The student may request time out of the room for 10 - 15 minutes that will be spent in a supervised area- the office, counselor's office, library, etc.

Limit the TIME OUT opportunities, if necessary, for a student who abuses it. Limiting the number of times is also effective with the Emotionally Disturbed student, because, he/she can leave the room before he/she becomes very disruptive, but will be careful to make the number of TIME OUTS last all day.

Seek student input - let students feel some "control" over the situation.

Allow student choices or decision making opportunities on how they will accomplish the task.

Be firm but not harsh.

Do NOT set forth ultimatums. The student will "test" you just to see what you will really do. Act as if the entire situation is UP TO THE STUDENT and express CONCERN for the student's choice.

PREVENTIVE MEASURES FOR STUDENTS WHO SEEK REVENGE

Show you care for the student BEFORE there is a problem.

Let EACH student know you consider him/her a friend (or someone special). Students usually do not seek revenge if they feel the person cares about them.

Let the students verbalize "upsetting" experiences. LISTEN to them.

If you do not have the time to listen, ASK the student to write you a BRIEF note about it.

If the student tends to "tattle" on everyone, let the student put his/her report (tattling) in writing. REQUIRE that it be at least one full page in order for you to have all the facts. This will discourage tattling. They will not want to write a long report in order to tell you something.

Be sensitive to each student's needs and feelings.

Allow students to express "unhappiness" in ways other than verbal communications - drawings or written work or telling stories "about someone they know."

Use sincere and specific praise when appropriate.

Provide the student with opportunities to talk to you (other than the lesson).

Avoid negative remarks.

Avoid situations that may embarrass a student.

Treat students with respect.

Try to understand their side when they talk to you.

IV.

RIGHT CHOICE
IMPLEMENTATION

RIGHT CHOICE IMPLEMENTATION

This program is designed to give attention to the well-behaved students and to promote excitement about being good.

It focuses on teaching the students decision making skills in discipline and concepts of socially acceptable behavior.

It empowers the students to become responsible for their own behavior.

The main components are:

The program is based on the belief that life is a series of CHOICES. Every minute of the day, we CHOOSE; but with those CHOICES comes responsibilities and consequences.

The program works only to the extent that the teacher works for its success.

TEACHING and PRACTICING are a MUST.

Fairness and consistency are essential.

GETTING THE STUDENTS STARTED

First:

Tell the students that many exciting things have been planned for the well-behaved students.

Explain that you are beginning a new program called Right Choice and they will be in charge of their own conduct.

Really stress that THEY WILL CHOOSE WHAT THEY DO, BUT THEY WILL BE RESPONSIBLE FOR THOSE CHOICES.

THEY will be THE ONE GIVING THEMSELVES consequences - good or not so good, depending on what they CHOOSE to do.

Let them know that you believe that they are smart enough to CHOOSE GOOD consequences for themselves.

Second:

Set aside about 20 - 30 minutes any time during the day for the first two or three weeks to TEACH AND PRACTICE procedures, class routines, and social skills.

Practice over and over until they do not have to be monitored closely.

The teacher and students determine class rules. (Samples are in the last section of this book.)

It is better to have a few rules - well kept, than a long list that is burdensome to monitor.

After the first few weeks, it takes only about 5 - 10 minutes a day to teach the lessons.

It is recommended that students be given two weeks "to practice" before the consequences begin. REMIND THEM DAILY THAT THEY ARE PRACTICING. Let them know that SOON consequences will begin.

Let them know the EXACT DAY that consequences begin. Be SURE they understand!

Let them know the types of things that they will be CHOOSING as consequences.

EXAMPLE: Fighting - Two hours of detention!
            Name calling - Write 40 DIFFERENT nice
            things about the other person.
            Talking - Loss of FREE TIME.

DISCUSS CONSEQUENCES A LOT BEFORE THEY ARE CHOSEN BY THE STUDENTS. They REALLY need to understand that it is their CHOICE!

Consequences are good as a deterrent ONLY if they are TOUGH!

Third:

The lessons are presented as prompts and suggestions to teach the concepts of social skills.

The students need to know the definition and main concepts presented.

The teacher should teach one lesson each week.

There are 31 lessons. Many schools may elect to teach five lessons and then do one week of review over those five (for distributive education).

Other teachers may prefer to teach all 31 and then review the areas most needed by their school.

Another choice is to spend two weeks at the time of instruction on areas that the students have a great deal of problems. You may spend more weeks on "Tattling Versus Reporting" or "Name Calling and Fighting."

Longer time spent on the study of "Cultures" could be combined with a Social Studies Unit and end with a program or pageant.

The content of the lessons is flexible. The lessons are not divided into "days" for teaching. The teacher determines what her class needs and how much to present at a time.

The format of the lessons is "teacher friendly" and written so that the teacher can easily glance at the book as he teaches and follow the concept without extensive preparation.

There is no set order that must be followed in teaching. Of course, it is STRONGLY RECOMMENDED that the first three be taught first and in the order in which they are presented here.

These lessons lay the foundation for future work on Right Choice.

Fourth:

In teaching discipline, it is ESSENTIAL that teachers keep in mind the students' various "methods/styles of learning" not to be confused with "discipline."

Some students want to know "reasons" for learning. They do not see the need to work unless they know the importance of the activity. (Does this count for a grade?)

Other students learn in an orderly manner and want ALL instruction and directions presented in that manner. They first want to know what "Step -by - Step" procedures they should follow. They like it best if the teacher presents ALL information in that fashion.

There are also those who focus on "How About..." They are creative and want to put their own ideas into an activity. They do not want to be given step - by - step (to follow in detail) assignments. They do not always recognize this creativity in themselves and truly "believe" that they followed the directions (when they really "added their own touch").

Another group of students are only concerned about "Getting It Done." They want to do it now - often, not even waiting for all the directions from the teacher. Therefore, they want the directions repeated when it is time to start. They also can be found turning "to the back part of the book" - ready to "get on to the next thing,"

These, combined with "left brain and right brain" along with tactile, auditory, and visual learning, create an awesome task for the teacher.

Students need to be TAUGHT how to "deal with" their methods of learning. It takes time for some of them to learn to comply with rules and expectations.

A variety of activities along with SOME areas for student "choices" (at least sometimes), both in selecting and in how to complete the assignment, will result in meeting more needs of the students.

Be careful that some of these learning methods and needs are not mistaken for discipline problems. Such problems could "look like" refusal to follow directions - when maybe they thought that they did. Or, not paying attention - when they really thought they were.

Often, it is hard to tell the difference, but getting to know the students helps.

It is just well to be aware that there are so many components involved in learning and teaching. The teachers who make allowances for these styles and needs will certainly be successful with discipline.

PRAISE, RECOGNITION, AND ACTIVITIES

People in general respond to praise, recognition, and rewards. Students feel good about themselves when they are the ones receiving these.

Some activates that can be done daily are:

Give SPECIFIC praise to all students.
Encourage them to do well.
Each teacher may decide how he/she will give praise and recognition in the classroom.

Recognition suggestions:

Free time - earned sometimes by individual
Turn to sit in teacher's chair
Leader of the line
Sit by friend at lunch
Select position of desk in class
Good note to parents
Good phone call to parent
Visit to principal for praise or sticker
One homework pass
Add student's name to Principal's Brag Book
Teacher helper
Messenger
Group activity leader
Ten minutes to read in the library
Wear button (showing good conduct or effort)
Lead pledge or other class activity
Certificate of Recognition (Black line masters included at back of this book.)
Coupons - (Black line masters for coupons in back of this book.)

Coupons can be used for small items in drawing held weekly.
Coupons can be used to "cash in" for one of the above.

    Example: 25 coupons - Sit in
                     teacher's chair for 15 minutes.
                     30 coupons - Line leader
                     50 coupons - One homework pass

Give coupons freely for good conduct and effort. (Lunch "baggies" are great for saving coupons.)

Allow students to think of things for which they are willing to earn coupons.

Adults want to get their paycheck for hard work. These can be considered "paychecks." Students need to learn that hard work pays. Indeed, you often do good things because you are a good person, but in the every day run of life, you get back what you invest.

END OF SIX WEEKS ACTIVITIES

The underlying basic concept is to teach students that they are responsible for their conduct. They CHOOSE. When they choose to do good things then good things will happen for them, One of those good things is the end of the six weeks (or three weeks) activity.

The students need to be told ahead of time that they can earn attending and/or participating in a fun activity at the end of the six weeks.

Some teachers may wish to post the names of Right Choice students in the hallways.

Put the teacher's name at the top of the list and the teacher will add the students' names as they "earn" the right to be listed.

The list may be changed each six weeks. Names may be added daily or anytime that the teacher determines that a student has earned the honor.

Names may be taken off at any time that wrong choices are made.

Grade levels need to set the criteria for their students. Kinder MAY be more tolerable. Fifth grade may feel that students who have "A" or "B" in conduct deserve to be considered Right Choice. First grade may want to allow one "C" for the six weeks.

While this is a teacher decision, remember the MORE you require in good discipline, the MORE you will get. Set your standards high, but not too high. You may consider "raising" the expectation for the second semester. If you do, tell the students ahead of time.

Remind the students that THEY CHOSE NOT TO GO. Get excited about the Right Choice activity. They will get excited about attending.

SUGGESTIONS FOR ACTIVITIES

Teacher Volleyball Game	Lower grades may watch. Upper grades may play against the teacher. Draw students names to decide who plays - others watch.
Talent Show	Students may attend or be in it.
Teacher Baseball Game	Same as above.
Play or Program	Put on by one grade.
Puppet Show	Students or Professional
Magic Show	Professional or by students
Clown	With short talk about Right Choice
Video	Of some literary value
Game Board Festival	Students bring game boards (or puzzles). Use gym and lunch room -or outside for 30 minutes of fun.
Free Time	30 minutes to play with friends outside
Teacher Talent Show	A favorite!!!

Fun Time	Have several activities planned. Students select which to attend. Finger paint, Fossil making, musical parade around school and the grounds, Drama, Story Time, etc.
Field Trip	Notify parents ahead of time that their child will CHOOSE TO GO OR NOT. GET THE PARENTS TO SIGN THE NOTICE AND RETURN IT. (Some students CHOOSE to be deprived of the EDUCATIONAL OPPORTUNITY IN CLASS BY THEIR off task behavior, so they ALSO refuse the field trip opportunity by CHOICE.)
Kite or Airplane Flying Time	Students make and fly! Great for spring! Best scheduled one grade at a time.
School Picnic	Eat outside or other area.
Sports Fun Game	Fun activity planned for outside or gym.
Eat in Classroom with teacher	Students love it. Some schools use this EVERY THREE WEEKS. (Other students stay in lunch room under supervision.)
School Carnival	Fun activities to take part in (not prizes) Parents may help.

These are only suggestions. Students or your teachers may have something else they really want to do.

Be creative! Have fun with the students! Encourage all students to CHOOSE TO GO.

SUCCESS FOR RIGHT CHOICE DEPENDS ON:

Students knowing their CHOICES and UNDERSTANDING WHY AND HOW to make Right Choices.
Teachers taking time DAILY TO TEACH the concepts.
Teachers providing practice time.
Teachers REALLY CARING ENOUGH TO HELP ALL STUDENT IMPROVE.
LIFE IS CHOICES, LEARN TO MAKE GOOD ONES!

V.

RIGHT CHOICE LESSONS

CHOICES

OBJECTIVE: To teach the student that life is made up of a series of choices and he needs to develop an understanding of the relationship between his actions (choices) and consequences or results of those actions.

EXPECTATION: The child will be aware that he chooses what he says or does and must accept resulting consequences.

DEFINITION: You decide, you pick, you make decisions about what you will do.

DISCUSSION: When choices are discussed a list may be made on the chalkboard, overhead, or chart of the ideas presented.

What are the results of your choices?

Right Choices:
Good feelings about yourself
Praise
Learn lessons

Stay healthy
Get along with others
Have friends
Be liked
Parents pleased with you

Wrong choices:
Cause trouble
Be corrected
Punished
Not liked
Bad reputation
Poor grades on lessons
Poor grade in conduct

What other ideas can students add to either list?

Your life depends on the choices you make every minute.
Such as: Eat healthy - To have good health.
Watch for cars in traffic - To stay safe.
Exercise - To have a healthy body.
Study - To learn your lessons.

Can you name other things that the type of choice you make determines what happens to you?

Why should you make good choices?

To feel good about yourself
To be a good citizen
To act mature (grown up)
To make living around others nicer
To get along well with others
To keep from causing problems
To have others be happy to be around you
To set a good example

To keep from causing other people problems

Name some things that happen in school in which you have choices.

Prompts: To do your lessons
To listen to your teacher
To do what others are doing (good or otherwise)
To follow the rules
To study
To work hard enough to finish on time
To be responsible for yourself
To be friendly
To act happy

Remember: There is POWER in choosing. If you follow other students, you are giving them power over you. Is that what you want?

Would you rather be in charge of yourself?

Your choices often affect others.
Example: Peer pressure!

Important fact -
Peer pressure means that you put pressure on yourself to please your peers.
Your peers do not "PUT" pressure on you.
You CHOOSE to pressure yourself into pleasing them.
The more times you CHOOSE to "do just anything" to please your peers the more they will expect it of you.

Adults have authority over students who are under their supervision. Listening to them is different from listening to other students.

Make a list of examples of good choices.
Following school rules

Obeying adults
Being friendly
Using good manners
Being polite to others
Completing your school work
Doing jobs at home, school, or elsewhere
Taking turns
Smiling and being happy

Why don't you make right choices all the time?

It is hard to do so.
It is especially hard to do so EVERY time.
Sometimes, you just don't feel like it.
Sometimes, you make wrong choices to get attention,
(But, it gets the wrong kind of attention.)
Sometimes, the wrong choice seems easier to do.
Sometimes, you do not take time to consider what the
results will be.

Can you think of other reasons why you do not make right choices
sometimes?

When can you blame others for what you did or said? Never!!!!!!

Statements such as: "He made me do it," or "She told me to," do not take
away responsibility from you for your actions.

You CHOSE to listen to that person. It was still your choice.

ACTIVITY:

Let each student tell of one good choice he made
recently.
Name some things that would be wrong choices.

Let the class decide on one choice that would be good for the class.

Let the class keep a chart for one week to monitor how well they keep the choice.

Suggestions for choice:

Line up without being corrected.

Super good conduct during restroom time.

All materials ready on time.

Entire reading (or other) lesson without someone disrupting.

Friendly, cooperative group work.

Excellent conduct at lunch.

What other choices could be chosen?

Note: CHOICE is the major component of this program.

Students need to be reminded DAILY that THEY CHOOSE!

PURPOSE OF RULES

OBJECTIVE: To help students realize that rules serve a purpose in our lives.

EXPECTATION: Students will more fully comprehend that in order to live peacefully we need to keep rules.

DEFINITION: A rule is something that tells you what to do or not to do.

EXAMPLE: There is a rule that you do not speak in class unless you raise your hand and wait to be called on to speak.
Purpose of the rule: To keep order in the class.

How does keeping order help the class?

EXAMPLE: When you keep order in the class, you can be sure that everyone can listen to the person speaking.

Name three or four other school rules.

Why do you think the rule is good? Could the school do without the rule?

Can you think of a rule that would be good to make for your class?

Why would it be good?

Do people have rules in their homes?

Prompts:

Keep your room clean.
Do not stand on the furniture.
Pick up your things when you finish using them.
Do not slam the door.
Do not talk to strangers.
Go to bed on time.

Can you think of others?

Are there other places that have rules besides home and school?

Prompts:

Businesses
Signs that say: No shirt, no shoes, no service.

Signs that say: If you break it, you buy it.

Government
Stop at the red light.
Pay your taxes.
Do not steal.
Children must go to school. Yes, that is a government rule. Is it a good one? Why?

Can you tell rules for these?

    Hospitals
    Libraries
    Sports
    Amusement Parks
    Buses
    Theaters

Can you think of others?

    Can you give reasons why each of the rules you talked about is good?

Who is helped by the rules
    in the homes?
    in businesses?
    in government?
    in theaters?
    in hospitals?

When do you find rules hard to follow?

What about rules in playing games?
    Are they hard to follow?
    Why?

When are rules the hardest to follow?

    When you do not feel like it!
        Sometimes, you do not have trouble following the rules because you are in a good mood. But, sometimes you just do not feel like doing it.

        It is also REAL hard to follow rules when you see someone else NOT following the rule and nothing seems to happen to that person. You think, if he/she can do that so can I.

It is hard to make right choices when others do not!

ACTIVITY:

Have students work in groups and decide which two class rules are the most important to them.

Let them present their choices to the class and explain why they chose them.

Let them decide who has the best idea and how the class can monitor the rules they decide are the best for them.

SUGGESTION:

Put a paper clip (or other small object) in a jar or box for every class period (reading time, math time, etc.) that the class keeps the rules during that time.
Plan a fun activity for the day that the jar or box is full or reaches a certain number.

A fun activity could be hearing a good book read to them, five or ten minutes free time, or a few minutes to play a classroom game.

Spend a few minutes to discuss the progress that the class is making. Is there anything the class can do to help those having trouble keeping the rules? Be more encouraging to them? Take a minute to give them attention? Will these help?

Why don't you like rules?

You do. But, you find them hard to keep all the time. Even when you have trouble keeping the rules, you think that others should keep them or receive a consequence. When you get caught breaking a rule, you want everyone else who broke a rule to be in trouble also. But, when you do not get caught, you do not tell on yourself. That is all right, but you have to take correction without complaining when you ARE caught.

Better yet, try to remember that EVERY TIME you CHOOSE to break a rule you are taking a chance of being caught!

Work at not breaking the rules!

RESPONSIBILITY

OBJECTIVE: To teach students that they are responsible for their actions.

EXPECTATION: Students will learn how to act in a more mature manner.

DEFINITION: Responsibility means you are the one who has to be sure that something is done.

EXAMPLE: At home if you are responsible for picking up your toys, then you must be sure that the toys are put away properly.

You are also responsible for things other than helping at home. One of the most important things you are responsible for is how you act wherever you are.

EXAMPLE: You get upset because the teacher does not let you be first in line.
You are responsible for acting nicely, even when you do not get what you want.

> If someone says something "ugly" to you, you are responsible for how you answer. Even though that person was not nice, you can choose to be nice. It will be HARD to be nice to someone who is not nice to you.

Others choose the way they act. They are responsible for what they do. But, regardless of how they act, you have a responsibility to choose for yourself how you act.

Things you are responsible for in school include such things as:

Having your school supplies ready.
Studying your lessons.
Having your work finished on time.
Doing your homework and turning it in.
Listening to the teacher in class.
Following directions.
Obeying rules.
Making friends and/or getting along with others.

Discuss what you have to do with each of the above areas to be a responsible person.

PROMPTS:

Area - supplies.

Your responsibility	Have your supplies ready and keep them neatly in assigned place.
	Have them ready to use.
	Get more from home when needed.

Continue this type of discussion for each or discuss others that the class may wish to address.

Remember: You can not hold someone else responsible for what you should do.

Such as: My mother forgot to help me with my homework.
               My mother didn't put my homework in my school bag.
               My mother forgot to remind me to do my homework.

You have to train yourself to remember and be responsible.

Why is it important to become responsible?

Because if you do not work on it now, you will not be a responsible person as an adult.

Also, when you are a responsible person life is better.

Others know that they can depend on you.

If you feel it is too hard to always be responsible, remember, you always come to school with your shoes on your feet. There has probably never been a child who had to call home for mother to bring their shoes that he/she forgot to wear to school!

Since you do not come to school barefoot, when you put your shoes on in the morning, use that time to remind yourself about your homework, notes, or other things that you need to bring to school.

You could also make up other ways of remembering things that you are responsible for doing.

When you are growing up you need to learn that everyone needs to do his/her part.

ACTIVITY:

Make copies of the following puzzle.
Cut them into pieces.
Put students in to small groups.
Give each group one set of puzzle pieces.
Each student gets two or three pieces that they are responsible for putting in the proper place to complete the puzzle.

They may NOT SPEAK WHILE WORKING!
No one may tell another where to place his/her piece.
Each child is responsible for what he has.

When the puzzle is complete let them discuss how they felt being completely responsible.

How did those who wanted to "do" for the others in the group feel?

It takes a lot of HARD work to learn to become a responsible person.

You can if you CHOOSE!

PUZZLE - Run copies and cut into pieces.

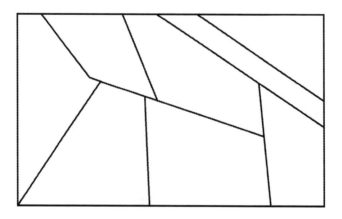

ATTITUDE

OBJECTIVE:	To help students develop wholesome attitudes and concepts about self and life.
EXPECTATION:	Students will realize that attitudes can be positive if they work toward understanding themselves as well as others.
DEFINITION:	It is the way you FEEL about things. Your actions and facial expressions sometimes "show" your attitude. They show how you feel.
EXAMPLE:	If you hate math, you can do math without ACTING like it is awful or complaining about it. You can avoid making faces or complaining every time you have to do math. It also includes not talking in an impolite manner such as "How should I know?" or "So?"

When you talk rudely or act impolitely because you are not enjoying something then people know that you have a bad attitude about it.

Does this mean you have to like everything? NO!

Jeanette Bradley M. Ed.

Is it wrong not to like something? NO!

It is natural not to like some things or some people, but you can TRY to act nicely or "put up" with it the best way that you can.

You can't always change how you feel, but you can work on controlling how you act about it.

    EXAMPLE: If you hate language class you can:

                    SMILE - Smile and act like it's not so bad. Do the work without complaining. Keep from making faces, even frowning. Be sure not to interrupt the class. Be sure not to bother someone next to you.

                    Try to think of at least ONE thing you do like about it. (Example - You do not have language all day - it is only for PART of the day!)

Working to improve your attitude is a VARY HARD thing to do.

It will take a lot of effort, but it can be done.

Making these right choices will help you have a good attitude about something that you do not like.

This does NOT mean that you will start LIKING it, but you will not spend your time thinking about how much you dislike it.

If you do not spend some time to improve your attitude, it will usually get worse.

Will your attitude get better immediately? NO! But if you work on it, it will slowly improve. Remember - This is VERY HARD to do, but you can succeed if you try.

Working on a bad attitude is a real sign of growing up.

Often, adults have to control their attitude to keep their job. Some day your job may depend on your good attitude.

SMILE - A smile is the best way to begin work on a bad attitude. Try, everyone can smile!

ACTIVITY: Make a BIG smiley face on a poster (or on a bulletin board) and let students put their initials on it each day that they show a good attitude.

If the class wants, they can individually or as a group, decide on one "hard" time of the day to improve. If most students have trouble with P.E., then pick that time to improve - or it may be lunch time that needs improving.

At the end of the week (or two weeks), count how many initials are on the poster.

Plan a few minutes of fun time to celebrate success.

Check with another class and see who had the most initials.

ACTIVITY:

Put the students into small groups.
Let them decide on two or three things that usually cause bad attitudes.

Discuss how to make things better.

or

List two or three things on the board that usually cause bad attitudes and let the students discuss how to make things better. Let each group report back to the class.

EXAMPLE:

Things that usually cause bad attitudes:

You do not get your way (in playing or working on a project) so you "hate" the activity.

You are not good at something (art, sports, math) so you "hate" it.

You feel that you do not get enough attention so, you hate it when others get attention.

You do not like taking turns unless you are first.

After discussing these, let students offer other things that may cause a bad attitude.

REMEMBER: It is natural to dislike some things.

Attitude is your FEELINGS about something and SHOWING how you feel to others by the way you act.

To have a positive attitude it is necessary to try "to make the best" of those things or situations that we do not like.

ANGER

OBJECTIVE: To help students understand that anger is a natural thing which can happen to anyone.

EXPECTATION: Students will know skills to use when dealing with anger.

DEFINITION: Anger is the bad or upset feeling you have when someone does something you do not like.

Is it all right to feel anger?

   Yes, it is natural. In fact, sometimes, you get upset or angry when someone just walks by your desk or touches something of yours.

   Sometimes, "they just look at you" and you are angry about it.

If it is O.K. to get angry why worry about it?

   It is not getting angry that is the problem. It is what you do when you are angry that you have to worry about.

What can you do when you get angry?

Ask the teacher (or the adult who is there) for COOL OFF time, (time by yourself).

Move a little bit away by yourself.

Breath in and out deeply and slowly. It will help you calm down.

Remind yourself, you want to make a right choice.

Remind yourself, you will feel better in a little while.

Think about exactly what made you angry and how it could have been prevented. Did you cause it to happen? (This may be a HARD fact to accept.)

After CALM DOWN TIME:

Talk about your problem with the adult (teacher, principal, counselor, or nurse) who is with you.

Explain what happened.
Explain why it upset you.
Be honest. This part is hard. You may have accidently caused part of your own problem. That can happen.

You may have caused the other person to be angry.

Listen to what the other student has to say.
It may not have been on purpose. He/She may not know that what happened upset you.

Work with the adult to reach a solution to make the situation better.

Be willing to apologize or to accept an apology.

When you are angry DO NOT:

> Call names.
> Hit, shove, push or do anything to hurt.
> Make threats - (Such as, "I'll get you after school.")
> Think that the other person is the ONLY one at fault.
> Think that you had a "right" to hit or push.
> (Adults at school are there to help protect you.)

Remember - AVOID OR BACK OFF FROM:

> A person
> A situation
> Or something that was said or happened that made you angry.

Remember:

> They can not make you DO something you do not CHOOSE to do.
> What you do when you get angry is your choice.

IF YOU SAY:

> "He made me do it."
> "He made me fight."
> "She told me to lie."

You are simply trying to find a way to get the blame off of yourself.

> NO ONE MAKES YOU!
> YOU CHOOSE!

If they are bad, you can still CHOOSE to do the RIGHT thing.

WHY CHOOSE NOT TO FIGHT OR NAME CALL BACK?

1. It shows you are more mature.

You would expect a two year old to cry and fuss if you accidently caused his/her drink to get spilt.

But -

You would be shocked to see a grown man cry and fuss in a store if his drink were accidently spilt.

You do not mature (act grown up) automatically. You need to work at making Right Choices that are hard.

2. It will not solve anything to fight or call names.
Some students (and even some adults) like to call names, swear (say bad words) and fight.
They think their anger is a "good reason" to do these things.
Anger is NOT a good reason to do these things.

3. Fighting gives you a bad reputation.
4. Best of all - You will feel good about yourself if you make Right Choices.
5. Most people regret hurting others because of anger. Try to avoid what you will regret later.
6. Think about the consequences for hitting or pushing. Consequences can be tough. Will it be worth the consequence? (Some students think it is worth taking the consequence to get to hit or push and then change their mind when it it time to do the consequence!)

Everyone feels anger at some time and you are the only one who can deal with yours.

REMEMBER: COOL OFF -CALM DOWN- before you act!
                        Think about what will happen next!
                        Think about how the situation can be made better.

Use talking about the problem to try to solve the problem.

Think about the consequences!
Act mature! VERY HARD TO DO!

Make the Right Choice! Also hard, at times.

ANGER IS NOT A REASON TO MAKE WRONG CHOICES.

ACTIVITY: Draw a tree on a large piece of paper.

On each branch put something that causes you to get angry.

DISCUSS: How long can a tree grow and still be pulled out of the ground by hand?
3 weeks?
1 month?
6 months?
1 year?

If it has a problem, will it come up easily?

How long can a bad habit (such as hitting when you are angry) "grow" and then be gotten rid of later?

The longer the tree grows the harder it will be to pull it up.

The longer you are angry the harder it will be to control your anger.

PRIDE IN SELF AND SCHOOL

OBJECTIVE: To instill pride in students for themselves and their school.

EXPECTATION: Students will know reasons to have pride in self and school.

DEFINITION: A reasonable amount of self-respect.
A good feeling about some possession or something that you do.

EXAMPLE: You feel proud of your family because they are good people.
You feel proud of your favorite ball team when they try hard (and sometimes win).
You are proud of your school because it is one of the best.

When should you feel proud of yourself?

Let students contribute their ideas.

PROMPTS: When you try hard.
                      When you make good grades.
                      When you make right choices.
                      When you help others.
                      When you behave.

Let students add to the list. You may want to make a list on a chart or the chalkboard.

When should you feel proud of your school?
All the time, because the students ARE "the school!"

The students study, listen, work, and behave. So everyone, parents, teachers, friends, and other students are proud of them.

When the students do a good job, everyone says things like, "Your school is great!"

When the students' scores are high (in both lessons and sports), everyone says things like, "Your school is a wonderful school!"

When the students are well behaved, people say things like, "Your school is a terrific place."

You, the students ARE the school!

Knowing good things about your school and good things about yourself will help you feel proud of both.

What good things do you know about yourself?

Prompts: Your desk and supplies are kept neat.
                      You get along well with others.
                      You say nice things about others.
                      You always have your work finished on time.
                      You always do your homework.

You try hard in sports.

You have a sense of humor - you can take a joke.

You are polite.

You study for tests.

You pay attention in class.

You are willing to help others.

You are willing to accept an apology.

How many more can you list?

Pride in yourself means a REASONABLE amount of FEELING GOOD ABOUT YOURSELF.

That means you see the good things that you do.

It does not mean that you see yourself better than everyone else.

To be proud of your talents and achievements is a good thing.

It is acceptable to say things like:

Yes, I sing well. I'm in the choir.

I won second place in the race!

My art picture won a blue ribbon.

I make all A's on my report card.

I am smart and I work hard. I do well in math.

When you try and/or work hard, it is great to feel good about yourself.

While it is great to feel proud of yourself, be sure to avoid talking about yourself TOO MUCH of the time. Others will get tired of it and it will begin to sound like bragging.

Bragging is considering yourself to be BETTER than others. Too much talk about yourself WILL sound like bragging.

Everyone has some things that they do better than others. Think about yourself and decide what is your best talent or achievement and enjoy doing it well!

Knowing good things about yourself and good things about your school will help you feel proud of both.

ACTIVITIES:

List things that you are proud of in your school.

List things that you are proud of in yourself.

The following may be a large or small group activity.

Make banners with slogans that show how proud you are of yourself and your school. This could be done on any type of paper.

Examples of slogans:

Just can't hide that (school name) pride.

(School name) best in the state!

Look at the rest.

You'll see (school) is the best.

We study! We shine! We succeed!

#1 Students! #1 Staff! #1 School #1 Forever!

Display the banners in the hall.

DO WITH THEM?

PROBLEMS - WHAT TO DO WITH THEM?

OBJECTIVE: To teach students how to recognize problems in their life.

EXPECTATION: Students will be better at recognizing problems and understanding that they can not always control what happens.

DEFINITION: A problem is something that bothers you because you do not like what is happening.

EXAMPLE: Someone often calls you names you do not like.

PROBLEM SOLVING:

                   DO NOT call names back. You would be acting as badly as the person that is doing it.

DO NOT DO SOMETHING WORSE - LIKE HIT OR PUSH. That will surely make the problem worse.

DO NOT get others to help you get even. That will also make the problem worse.

Blaming others will not make a problem better.

GOOD SOLUTIONS: Think about your problem carefully to know EXACTLY why it is a problem. Did you give the person a reason to to call you names?

Is it a problem all of the time or just some of the time?

Think about things you have already done to make it better and try to decide why they did not work.

Talk to an adult about the problem. Be sure to give ALL the facts - not just your side.

Ask the person why he is bothering you.

Or ignore the person (HARD TO DO, but if you really ignore him, he will eventually get tired of it and leave you alone).

Jeanette Bradley M. Ed.

If you accidentally did something to start the problem, APOLOGIZE!!!! An apology can do a great deal to solve problems.

Sometimes, you may ACCIDENTALLY bump, step on, push, or trip over someone. That person will FEEL INJURED. It is VERY IMPORTANT for you to apologize IMMEDIATELY. Your apology will tell that person that you did not mean to hurt him. If you do not apologize, the person will probably feel that it was on purpose.

Likewise, when another person accidentally bumps or pushes you be sure to accept his apology! (Just as you want your apology to be accepted!)

If your problem deals with lessons, rules, or other school matters, talk with an adult. Your parents, teachers, the counselor, the nurse, or the principal will all be willing to help you.

REMEMBER:
Talking may not solve the problem, but it will probably give you some ideas about what to do to make the situation better.

If your problem is that you did not get something done or did something that was wrong, then try the following:

Accept the fact that you made a wrong choice.
(This is VERY HARD to do.)
Do not lie! That will only make it worse.
Apologize.
Decide not to do it again and give your word that you will be better.
Then really make an effort to be better.

Everyone makes mistakes at one time or another, but the important thing is to LEARN from your mistakes.

It is not good to make mistakes and then to CONTINUE to make the same mistakes over and over.

If your problem is something that is happening at home, try to talk to your parents. If you can not talk to your parents, then talk to an adult at school, a teacher, the principal, the nurse, or the counselor.

Do not bring up your problem in the middle of class or in front of the other students. Ask to talk to an adult by yourself. Other students usually do not understand enough to help you.

Adults really do want to help.

Sometimes, when you try to make a problem better it only seems to get worse.

Be sure to give the situation time to get better.

Set a time during which you will focus on improving the situation.

For example: During the next two weeks, you will pay close attention to REALLY trying to improve the situation.

At the end of two weeks, check your progress. You may need an adult to help with this.

ACTIVITY:

Discuss problems that are common to many students. (AVOID SPECIFICS AND NAMES)

SUGGESTIONS FOR DISCUSSIONS:

Others do not like you
Low grades
Fights
Lying
Cheating

Picking on others - especially after school
Others call you names

Can you think of others?

Let students offer suggestions to make things better.

FREE TIME

OBJECTIVE: To give students an opportunity to practice social skills. Also to avoid their using instructional time to do so.

EXPECTATION: Students will not use instructional time to visit. They will use earned free time to do so.

DEFINITION: A few minutes (2-4) in which a student may choose what to do quietly - especially visit with class mates.

Students need time to visit with their friends.

Students need time to get to know others.

Students need time to tell something that they are "bursting" to tell.

Inform the students of the reasons that they will have free time once or twice a day.

Discuss that they will be CHOOSING to have free time by how much they stay on task during lessons to earn their free time.

Some teachers like to give two minutes at the end of each lesson (math, reading, etc.) others prefer to earn longer periods of time once or twice a day.

For example;

> Five minutes before lunch for the morning and five minutes before dismissal for the afternoon.
>
> Another option would be to give ten minutes in the afternoon.
>
> Fifteen/ twenty minutes on Friday is one more option.
>
> Let the class have some decision in what they want to earn.
>
> If only one or two (usually the same ones) are disruptive, let those students "sit out" the time earned and not participate. Avoid letting a few ruin it for everyone.

Discuss what may and may NOT be done during free time.

EXAMPLES:

> Students may (or may NOT) leave their desks.
> Students must speak quietly.
> Students may not leave the room without permission.
> Students will lose free time if they do not follow the rules (individually or as a group).

Students needed to be reminded OFTEN that they are the ones earning free time.

The best part about giving free time is that it has to be earned. They like it enough that they will work to have it.

If free time is "saved" for a longer time on Friday, then music or game boards may be added.

The teacher needs to set guide lines for the type of music and games allowed.

Reminder:

Free time does not really "take" from instructional time, because when students stay on task and do not cause interruptions, the teacher can complete instruction and have a few minutes for free time.

ACTIVITY:

Let students help make a list of things that will cause them to lose free time.

SUGGESTIONS:

Note writing
Wasting time
Visiting/talking during class
Disrupting the class
Incomplete work
Also, include the amount of free time the student will lose.

Make students aware that with free time they will not have to write notes or visit, or try to get someone's attention. They can do it during free time.

Since incomplete work will be finished during free time, they might as well complete their work and be able to visit during free time.

TATTLING VERSUS REPORTING

OBJECTIVE: To teach students that there is a difference between tattling and reporting.

EXPECTATION: Students will know when it is appropriate to tell the teacher something about someone and when it is not.

DEFINITION: Tattling is telling the teacher something that happened to get someone in trouble.
Reporting is telling the teacher something that can cause trouble, harm, or damage so that the teacher can help stop the problem.
The harm or damage may have already happened or it could be that someone is threatening to DO harm or damage,

EXAMPLE: Igor tells the teacher that Dison is playing with baseball cards and not working.
Of course, Igor wants the teacher to correct Dison.

That is tattling. There is no harm or danger involved.

It is the teacher's responsibility to OBSERVE and correct Dison. She will eventually notice Dison without Igor's help.

Lansi tells the teacher that several of the students are planning to beat up Jolee after school because Jolee missed the ball at P.E. time. They think that she made them lose the game. That is reporting.

Jolee is in danger of being hurt.

Before you tell the teacher something, ask yourself the following types of questions.

Will it help someone if you tell?
Will it prevent harm from happening?
Will it prevent damage?
Will it make a problem better?
Do you hope someone gets in trouble with the teacher?

If you really are doing it to help someone, it is reporting and a good thing to do.

Some of the types of things that should be reported are:

Fighting or plans for fights.
(Any aggressive act is considered fighting.
If an act LOOKS like fighting, it is TREATED like fighting.)
Demands for money, food, of personal things.
Demands for use of homework.
Students selling things at school.
Stealing.
Gangs and their activities.

Any damage to personal or school property.

Can the students add to this list?

Some types of tattling are:

> Arlof has a comic book.
> Dilan is looking out the window.
> Kayla is chewing gum.
> Lajune is out of her desk.
> Jamea took a cut in line.

IMPORTANT!　　When you report that someone hit you or called you an ugly name (or did some other harmful thing), BE REAL SURE that you get ALL of the facts straight.

EXAMPLE:　　If you tell the teacher that someone hit you, be REAL sure that you include what you did IF you gave that person a reason to be upset with you.

You have part of the guilt if you took that person's pencil (or did something else not nice) or called him an ugly name and were hit in return for your ugly act.

Sometimes, it happens that one student is rude or harmful to another and then several days later (even weeks later), the person decides to "get even."
By then, the offender has forgotten that he did something to provoke the issue.

Also, be sure to give your parents ALL the facts when you tell them that you are having trouble or problems with another student (or the teacher) at school.

When you leave out YOUR part, that information comes out later when your parents check with the teacher or principal and you are in trouble.

In conclusion - report ALL the facts - even your part.

It is IMPORTANT that you report serious matters. You have a right to be protected, so go to an adult for help.

ACTIVITY: Make a class list of things that are tattling.

Post the list in the classroom.

If someone tattles, that person has to do two nice things for the person that he/she tattled about in class.

Students may wish to suggest ways that the class can prevent tattling.

EFFORT

OBJECTIVE: To show students the importance of effort.

EXPECTATION: Students will realize that results depend on the amount of effort put into what is done.

DEFINITION: A serious attempt to do something.

Effort is hard because you try to get yourself to do something when you rather just do nothing.

People who are great became famous because they made an effort to do something special.

What effort did the following people make?

PROMPTS:

Columbus   Sailed to a new land
Washington   Worked hard to lead an army
Ben Franklin   Worked hard to invent things
Mary Lou Renton   Worked hard to win Olympics
Babe Ruth   Worked hard to be a great sport

Name some people who are famous and still working in their area of fame.

Who can you name in the following areas that have earned fame?

Music? Sports? Medicine? Science?

Inventions? Space? Entertainment? Politics?

Can you name people who are SUCCESSFUL (but maybe not famous) because of their efforts?

PROMPTS: Teachers, Parents, Students, Relatives, etc.

Did they have to make a big effort only one time?

Did they have to make an effort every, every day?

Name some of the things you do that take effort.

SUGGESTIONS:

You make an effort to:

Study
Listen in class
Complete work
Do homework
Clean you room
Use good manners
Be friendly
Make right choices

When you enjoy the lesson, it seems to take LESS effort because you want to do it.

It takes effort to make yourself do it when you do not enjoy it as much.

The actual "doing" (whether you want to or not) takes EFFORT.

Results of effort:

> When you make choices about effort, you need to think about the results you will get.

If you make an effort to study, what results will you get?

Results would include:

> Good grades
> Good feelings about yourself
> Good reputation
> Praise from parents/teachers

If you make an effort to be friendly, what results could you expect?

> More friends
> Others being friendly to you
> Good reputation.

What are other situations that require effort for good results?

Thinking about the results will usually help you make a better and more consistent effort.

Sometimes, when you really make an effort to improve, you do get better at that and then it does not seem to take as much effort as it did at first.

If you continue to work a little harder each day, it will slowly get easier.

Sometimes, it seems that you have to try REAL hard and others who seemingly do not try at all do better than you do.

That may indeed be true. Some people have talent in areas that you may not, and therefore need less effort to do the same as you (or maybe even better).

But, you are working for your own results - you are not necessarily focused on "showing someone up." Try to do your best for yourself.

Effort is hard! But you can choose to do anything you want to and with effort you can be successful.

Activity:

> Draw a picture of what you want to do or be in the near future or when you are grown up. On your picture, list some things that will require you to make an effort to attain.

Suggestions for now:
>> Play the piano
>> Run track
>> Speak another language
>> Be the best in math
>> Know how to cook
>> Know how to ride a bike

For the future:

>> Teacher
>> Politician
>> Pilot
>> Truck driver
>> Computer programmer

RIGHTS OF OTHERS

OBJECTIVE: To explore the concept of "rights."

EXPECTATION: Students will have an awareness of what rights are for themselves, as well as, for others.

DEFINITION: Everyone has the right to try to be happy, to own things, and to be protected from harm.

Let us take a look at these one at a time.

FIRST: The right to try to be happy.

Everyone wants to be happy. Being happy does not happen by itself. You have to work at being happy.

You are happy when you are pleased with yourself and what you are doing. Sometimes, this can mean doing what you do not like to do to get what you want.

EXAMPLE: You do not want to do your school work, but you do it because you will be happy that you are smarter and you will be happy that you are not in trouble for not doing your work.

EXAMPLE: You do not like to cook, but you cook, because you are happy when you have something good to eat.

What about others?

When you do things that make you happy, you must think about how it will effect others.

EXAMPLE: You like to be first in line. You can not be first if it is someone else's turn.

IMPORTANT: Our right to be happy can NOT get in the way of someone else's rights.

SECOND: You have the right to own things.

You have the right to own things and you are unhappy when someone ruins your things or takes them.

You love candy. Seranne has some. You can NOT take hers to make yourself happy.

What are some things that you own? Which ones would you be upset about if someone took them?

Someone's wrong choice could cause you to be unhappy.

If you take or ruin something that belongs to another person, you cause them to be unhappy. Your right to be happy can not cause others to be unhappy.

You must respect their rights!

THIRD: You have the right to be protected from harm.

You like to sit in the last desk. You can not shove Hiram out because you want that place. People do not have the right to harm others to get what they want.

If you are playing a game, you can not hit (or call ugly names) to get the ball or because you did not get the ball when you wanted it.

If someone hurts you, you do not do the same thing back to that person.

Report it to the teacher or any adult in charge. The adult will take care of the consequences. If you give a "shove for a shove," than you may also be in line for consequences.

It is VERY, VERY HARD not to hit or shove back. But, remember, if you do not, you will NOT receive a consequence. The other person will!!

You want to get even, but you must remember that it takes a better person to back off from trouble and to get adult help when it is needed.

You do not have to fight someone five years younger than you to prove that you are tough.

If you were asked you would probably reply, "I'm tougher than he is. I do not need to prove it."

If you feel you are NOT "tough," then you will want to fight.

Fighting will not make you tough. It may make you sore and if you "lose," you will be a "target" for others who want to "prove" themselves.

Cowards (losers) try to find other cowards to fight.

Only cowards fight to prove they are tough.

If you are REALLY tough, you do not have to prove it!

ACTIVITY: Make a list of the things students like to do and to have.

Let students select the ones most important to them.

Take the ones in which they showed the most interest and decide in cooperative groups what can be done to help protect the rights of others in each area selected.

Prompts for list of rights:
        To be happy
        To have fun
        To own things
        To be protected from harm
        To have friends
        To visit with friends
        To read good books
        To learn in school
        Not to be embarrassed
        To get attention
        To be successful

The activity needs to stress the idea that they have rights that they want others to respect.

They must also determine how they will respect the rights of others.

HONESTY / LIES

OBJECTIVE: To develop self-discipline in honesty.

EXPECTATION: Students will be aware of the importance of honesty in themselves.

DEFINITION: Honesty means telling the facts exactly as they happened.

When do we need to be honest?

> All the time:
> When talking to friends.
> When talking to teachers.
> When talking to neighbors.
> When talking to adults.
> When talking to other students.
> When talking to anyone.

Why do you need to be honest?

> Because you want:
> To feel proud (good) of yourself.

To be a good citizen.
To keep the facts straight.
To have a good reputation.
Others to trust you.

How can you be honest?

Tell exactly what you know.
Do not exaggerate - make the facts sound bigger or worse than they were.
Do not change any part.
Do not leave out any part.
Do not add anything to it.
Do not use gestures or "body language" (such as rolling your eyes) to add extra meaning to the facts.

OMISSION: Leaving out facts - on purpose - can be lying.

EXAMPLES: "I hit him because he hit me first!"
                   Leaving out the fact that you kicked him before he hit you.

                   Telling your parents, "The teacher picks on me."
                   Leaving out the fact that you did not stay in your desk and yelled out in class four times.

EVASION: Changing words can be lying.

EXAMPLES: "Did you hit him?"
                   You answer, "No."
                   When you actually SHOVED him hard.
                   Evading and avoiding answering to words can be lying because you are avoiding the truth.

Why do people lie?

They want:
To avoid punishment.
To try to hide what wrong choice they made.
To try to get someone else in trouble.
To try to make someone think that they are good.

They feel ashamed (bad) about what they did and do not want others to know.

What should be done when you make the wrong choices?

Be honest - HARD to do!
Accept the fact that you made a wrong choice.
Apologize for your wrong choice.
Decide to try to do better - HARD to do.
Do not try to "justify" your lie (give reasons to try to make what you did sound alright).

It is VERY HARD to admit you were doing something wrong, but lying just gets you in more trouble.

Sometimes, you may think that you will get out of trouble by telling a lie and then you become known as a liar! That gives you a bad reputation and it is hard to change a bad reputation.

What are the most important reasons to tell the truth?

To know for YOURSELF that you are being honest and trustworthy.
To grow up to be a good person.
To feel good about yourself and your actions.
Not to have to worry that you will be caught telling lies.
Not to have to worry about bad consequences.

ACTIVITY: Let students act out a skit.

The skit needs to deal with friends who are not honest with each other.

They may write their own or they may use the following suggestion.

Suggestion for one skit.

Emil and Igor are boys who are good friends.

On Saturday, Igor tells Emil that his mother grounded him and he can not play ball with him.

Later, that day Emil sees Igor at the mall with Guston.

On Monday, Igor tells Emil that he can not go to the park with him because he is working on some homework.

The next day, Emil hears Igor tell the teacher that he had to help his sick mother and could not do his homework.

Emil hears Tor whisper, "Igor and I played video games."

After the students act out the skit (or similar skits) discuss what happened.

DISCUSSION SUGGESTIONS:

> How did Emil feel?
> Will he believe Igor in the future?
> Did Igor care about Emil's feelings.
> Will an apology help Emil accept what Igor says?
> Did it happen too many times for Emil to believe Igor?
> How would you act if you were Emil?
> Will they be able to be friends again?
> Is someone REALLY a friend if they lie to you?

It is HARD to always tell the truth! But once you start telling lies, it is HARDER to get people to believe you even when your REALLY are telling the truth.

Work hard at ALWAYS telling the truth.

FAIRNESS

OBJECTIVE:	To teach students the concept of fairness.
EXPECTATION:	Students will have a better grasp of the meaning of fairness.
DEFINITION:	A just and equal treatment of all. It means not showing favoritism. It means following the rules.

Fairness is something you want for yourself, but not always for others.

EXAMPLE:	You want the teacher to be fair, but sometimes, you are not fair to the teacher.
	You want the other team to be fair, but sometimes, you aren't.
	You want rules to be fair, but sometimes, you do not follow the rules yourself.
	You want other students to treat YOU fairly, but sometimes, that is not what YOU do.

These make it sound as if being fair is HARD!

IT IS HARD!

What makes it hard is that when you are upset, or lose a game, or you are in trouble, you use "fairness" as a place to "place the blame."

EXAMPLES:　　　Your team lost so you say, "The other team did not play fair."

You get in trouble in class so you say something like, "The teacher is not fair," or "She picked on me."

You are upset so you say, "It's not fair."

If you are honest and fair, you would say such things as:

We lost the game. "The other team played hard."

You are in trouble. "I was not paying attention at the time."

You are upset. "I chose not to follow directions."

To be fair you need to be honest with YOURSELF.

You need to treat others as you want to be treated - FAIRLY!

You must recognize the fact that life is full of rules and you do not like some of them!

Not LIKING a rule does not mean that it is not a GOOD rule.

IMPORTANT!　　　Fairness does not always mean "EQUAL" in EVERY situation!

EXAMPLE: Members of a family do not eat the same amount of food. What is FAIR is for each member to get what he NEEDS. The mother is not considered unfair if she serves the father more than the smallest child in the family.

                         Likewise, the children in the family do not all eat EXACTLY the same amount. They eat what they need.

Along the same line:

    The teacher is fair if she gives each student the help in class (teaching and disciplining) that he NEEDS.

    For the MOST PART, students guilty of the same offense will (and should) receive the same consequence.

    In SOME instances, students guilty of the same offense do NOT NECESSARILY need the SAME consequence.

Consequences are given to BRING ABOUT A CHANGE IN BEHAVIOR not to "get even" with the student.

Therefore,   if one student is more likely to respond from being isolated and the other from detention after school, it would be FAIR if each received what he NEEDS TO IMPROVE.

                In giving different consequences, the students need to UNDERSTAND why they are receiving different consequences.

BEFORE something happens, that warrants consequences, INFORM the students that when they make wrong CHOICES they are CHOOSING A CONSEQUENCE. Let them know that consequences may not be the same. But, they will receive what THEY NEED TO GET BETTER.

Stress that they should be REAL careful not to CHOOSE a consequence; because, it will be tough and something they do NOT LIKE.

These concepts PROBABLY need to be stressed MANY TIMES for complete understanding.

IMPORTANT: The "AMOUNT/LENGTH" of the consequence should be CONSISTENT for all students according to age and offense.
(A first grader may receive a shorter or less consequence for the same offense that a fifth grader does.)

ACTIVITY: Let the students name people who need to be FAIR in their jobs and tell why.

PROMPTS: Athletes
Historians
Teachers
Judges
Jurors
Doctors
Parents

Can the students think of others?

It is HARD to be fair, but you can if you work at it.

FRIENDLINESS

OBJECTIVE: To teach the students how to be friendly.

EXPECTATION: Students will be made aware of ways to be friendly.

DEFINITION: Showing a kindly interest in someone or having good will toward them.

How can you act friendly?

Smile! That is the best thing you can do!
Treat others just as you want to be treated.
Talk nicely to others.
Listen to what they have to say.
Be happy around others.
Take turns talking and playing (in games).
Be forgiving if they do wrong. It is HARD to do, but you can.
Compliment others when they do something good.
Show how happy you are to see them.
Be loyal - do not repeat ugly things you may hear about your friends.
Be happy about good things that happen to your friends.
Offer to help (and then do so) when they have problems or more than they can do.

Spend time with them.
Invite them to join you in activities or fun.

A friend DOES NOT:

Always expect to have his way.
Expect to be the only friend. (You need all the friends you can get.)
Try to "boss" others.
Complain a lot.
Spread gossip.
Encourage you to dislike or not play with others.
Try to get you to do things that you should not.
Avoid being around you.

To have a friend, you must be a friend.

Sometimes, you have problems with your friends.

EXAMPLE OF PROBLEM:

It is hard to act like a friend when your friend does not pay attention to you.

POSSIBLE SOLUTION:

If your friend does not pay attention to you, spend time with someone else. Later, you can get back together with your friend.

Can you think of other possible solutions?

EXAMPLE OF PROBLEM:

It is hard to act like a friend when your friend forgets to act like a friend.

POSSIBLE SOLUTION:

Do not be rude because your friend was. Give him a chance to say he is sorry. Talk it over, and then try to be friends again.

Jeanette Bradley M. Ed.

Give the students time to discuss some of their problems with friends and how to handle the problems.

IMPORTANT! Before you begin this, establish a ground rule that the students MAY NOT mention names. If they "accidentally do" they will have to stop their discussion. BE FIRM with this. No one should be embarrassed in this discussion by having his or her name mentioned by someone else.

ACTIVITY:

Make a friendship chain around your room. On each paper chain write one character trait you would want a friend to have.

The chain can be as long as the students wish to make it.

When the chain is finished, read the words and try to have as many of the words in yourself as you can work on developing.

Being a good friend to many people is the best way to have many friends.

CULTURES

OBJECTIVE: To impart information about cultures so that students will develop an understanding and appreciation of other cultures.

EXPECTATION: Students will appreciate and accept the difference in cultures.

DEFINITION: Behavior typical of a particular group of people.

Discuss how life would be if:

People had just one kind of food. You had to eat that one food at every meal. (What food would you choose for that one food to be if you wanted to be healthy?)
Clothes were all one shape and the same color.
People all looked exactly alike.
People all talked the same way.
Everyone had to have the same kind of job.
Music could be played on only one kind of musical instrument.

Life would be boring!

You enjoy eating different foods.

You enjoy having different clothes.
You enjoy being able to tell people apart by the way that they look,
You like looking different.

So you should try to enjoy different cultures - different ways of saying and doing things.

Do not spend time trying to decide if one is better or not.

Spend time thinking how wonderful it is to get to learn about other people and their cultures.

You will probably enjoy some of their customs.

One interesting custom in Thailand is that they celebrate their New Year by throwing water on friends, visitors, and people passing by. They do so to bring rain during the next growing season. (Their New Year begins in April and it is usually a hot day so the water is welcome.) Would you enjoy this custom?

Why do some people not appreciate other customs and cultures?

It is usually because they do not understand why things are done.

When you take time to learn more about other cultures and customs, you can respect and/or accept the people of that culture easier through your knowledge and understanding.

Do you have to participate in their customs?

No - but you may enjoy it if you do.

Do you have to like their customs?

No - but you may like the person better if you know their customs better.

What are some ways to learn about different cultures and customs?

One of the easiest is to read about them in the school or public library.

Another way is to talk to people of other cultures.

When others offer information about their culture, offer information about your culture.

Exchanging information will benefit both sides.

ACTIVITY:

Make a large chart and list the different cultures of the students in your class (add extra cultures if you wish).

Your chart could be similar to the following example.

Nationality	Food	Holiday	Custom
North American	Hot Dogs	July 4th	Watch Fireworks
African/ American	Watermelon	June 19th	Picnic
Mexican	Taco/Tortilla	Cinco de Mayo	Parade

Let students add more information to the chart or make a similar chart with other nationalities. They may have to look up some information in the library or ask different people in the community to help complete the chart.

The key to accepting other cultures and customs is understanding. Try to learn all you can about other cultures.

NAME CALLING AND FIGHTING

OBJECTIVE: To show that name calling/fighting is a coward's way to try to solve problems.

EXPECTATION: Students will see that name calling and fighting are not necessary if they feel good about themselves.

DEFINITION: A coward is one who shows lack of confidence and feels a need to prove he is not afraid.

The definition of coward is given here, because a person who has self-confidence has NO NEED to name call or fight.

A person who is a coward tries to prove he is "tough" or "big stuff" by name calling or fighting.

A person who KNOWS he is tough has nothing to prove.

He does not need to name call!

He does not need to fight!

Name calling is done to make yourself SEEM better than someone else.

Racial slurs (saying something ugly about another person's race) are also a form of name calling aimed at making yourself seem better.

Fighting is done to prove you are not a coward, but if you are NOT a coward there is NOTHING TO PROVE.!

Since you are not a coward, nor do you want to be a coward, how can you settle a problem without name calling or fighting?

Find out what the other person thinks is the problem. He may have wrong facts.

Talking about it may give each side a better picture of the situation.

If you accidentally bothered the other person, APOLOGIZE IMMEDIATELY. Your immediate apology will let the other KNOW it was an accident!

If the other person wants to fight for "no reason," tell him that you have nothing to PROVE.

If someone wants to fight "to take you on" or because you supposedly offended him, do not accept. Seek adult help. Fighting will not solve anything.

If the other person calls names, IGNORE him. That type of person hates to be ignored. If he can not upset you, he will soon stop.

If a person wants to "USE YOU" to prove something to himself, do not let him do it.

If you can not solve your problems, and the name calling and threats to fight continue, you SHOULD report it to an adult - teacher, principal, counselor.

Name calling or fighting WILL NOT solve a problem.

Jeanette Bradley M. Ed.

Sometimes, the only way students can avoid name calling or fighting is to AVOID each other. That is better than choosing the tough consequences that happen as a result of name calling and/or fighting.

Remember, the CHOICE is YOURS. The other person can not MAKE you do anything.

Think about what you are choosing BEFORE you ACT.

Being CALLED a coward DOES NOT MAKE you a coward. It is HARDER to walk away than it is to name call or fight.

Defending yourself when you are NOT at school is different! AT SCHOOL, you need to let the teachers or other adults handle the problem if you can not without fighting.

When you are not at school or a school activity, then you need to follow what your parents advise you to do.

ACTIVITY:

Form a TOUGH GUY CLUB in your class. Only those who are not cowards may belong.

Anyone who calls names, shoves, hits, pushes, etc. is out of the club for a certain amount of time - determined by the class.

Plan a reward for the ones who can go the longest without being "out" of the club.

Weekly or bi-weekly allow the club members to meet for a few minutes to visit and encourage each other to stay tough.

Plan a fun activity for club members.

NOTE:

Defending yourself is not addressed here.

Many parents teach their child not to fight, but to defend himself, if necessary.

Many schools teach that at school the faculty is there to protect and defend students.

For the safety and welfare of the students, the schools SHOULD teach students that when students fight someone should get the teacher or an adult immediately. There is always an adult close by.

Students are told not to fight back. To do so will put "some" of the blame on that person.

The one who hits WILL receive a severe consequence. If both do some hitting, both will have a consequence.

The one starting it has the greater guilt and thereby chooses the tougher consequence by his/her choice to fight.

Name calling that leads to fighting is considered a SERIOUS OFFENSE.

IMPORTANT:
This lesson MUST be taught in accordance with the POLICY of the school where it is used.

VERY EFFECTIVE consequences must be in place for name calling and fighting.

As mentioned earlier, having the students write fifteen forty DIFFERENT sentences (depending on the grade level of the students) stating NICE things about the other students will help them know each other better and they will get along. Or, it will make them want to avoid each other not to get more NICE things to write.

It is effective to let them work together to find out "enough" nice things about each other.

Five o'clock detention is effective for fighting. Reminder: Detention is MOST effective if the student has to just sit. Work (reading also) makes the time go faster. They tend to watch the clock when they just sit. It makes the time go slowly.

If the name calling or fighting is repeated, then double the assignment. Warn them that they may not repeat any sentence that they have already used. (You will save the papers.) There could also be two days of detention.

RESPECT

RESPECT

OBJECTIVE: To teach the meaning of respect and the concept that people earn the respect of others.

EXPECTATION: Students will know when and how to show respect, as well as, how to earn respect from others.

DEFINITION: An act of giving special attention or having a high regard for someone or something.

Why is respect necessary?

Respect for others shows you have a high opinion of yourself and of others. You have high standards. Those who show respect receive respect.

Respect helps keep order. Authority keeps peace. Order and respect keep authority by choice instead of by force. We choose to have authority/rules and respect them. Some countries are ruled by force and fear, not by respect.

EXAMPLE: You should show respect for the president because he runs our country. You do not have to like him, but you show respect to him for the important position that he has.

What are some things and who are some people for which you should show respect?

Parents
Teachers, principals
Government officials - police, fireman, mayor, etc.
Ministers
Parents of friends
Show respect to the U. S. flag because it stands for our country - the greatest in the world.

How do you show respect?

Speak politely - the way you want others to speak to you.

Do not talk back to authority.

Have a positive attitude. Act like you accept the fact that someone is in charge of you. (Some one is in charge of the person who is in charge or you! Everyone has someone to whom they have to listen.)

Pay attention when they speak.

Do not damage things that have an important meaning - flag, monument, etc.

If you are too upset to speak politely, ask for time out (10-15 minutes should be allowed to any student requesting time out.) Calm yourself and then discuss your problem.

Life is not easy every day. You can make it better or worse by how you act. Being respectful tends to make the day better.

Do not try to be in charge of others. Many elementary students like to tell others what to do. "Get in line." "Put that down." "It's not your turn."

You also show respect for the privacy of others by not meddling (minding) in their business.

It is best to show respect for others by letting them be in charge of themselves.

Remember that you show respect when you treat a person or things in a special polite manner.

ACTIVITY: List the following statements on the board.

Who cares?
So what? or So?
I don't care.
I'm bored.
Big deal.
Who does he think he is anyway?
Why should I bother?
Yeah. So?

Let students write statements that would replace these and be respectful.

This should be a class activity with the statements written on a chart, chalkboard, or overhead projector.

DISCUSS: How would our country be without any respect?

How would our class be without any respect?

How would you act if the president visited us?

Isn't it important to treat others with respect also?

COURTESY

OBJECTIVE: To show how courtesy makes life more pleasant.

EXPECTATION: Students will know how to act courteously.

DEFINITION: Courtesy is the polite (nice) way that you treat others and others treat you.

Why is courtesy necessary?

Courtesy is necessary because:
It makes life more pleasant.
It shows respect for yourself as well as others.
It is a way to show friendliness.
It helps people get along better.
It shows you have a high standard of conduct.
It shows a willingness to get along with others.

How do you speak courteously?

You use words such as:

Please.
Thank you.
Pardon me.

Excuse me.
I appreciate your help.
I'm sorry.
It was nice or you to think of me.
May I please...

All of these are used at different times.

Discuss the times when it would be appropriate to use each one.

It is also considered courteous to speak to people when you see them.

It is nice to say things such as:

Good morning. Later, Good bye.
Hi, how are you?
Are you having a good day?
It is so good to see you.
How have you been?
It is so nice to see you.
Hello, how are things?

Can students think of other words that show courtesy?

Other ways that courtesy helps you are that it shows others that:

You are mannerly.
You have been taught well.
Your are mature.
You are educated.
You respect yourself.

Can you think of others?

If you are courteous and someone else is rude (not courteous in return), it means that you are the more mature (act "grown up") person because it is HARD to be polite to a rude person.

Jeanette Bradley M. Ed.

When someone shoves or yells something "ugly," you naturally want to do the same in return.

A mature, courteous person does not give back the same rude conduct.

He shows courtesy at all times. Yes, it is HARD, but you can do it if you practice.

If a two year old wants something and does not get it, he may yell and cry for it.

You would not cry or yell for something because you are too mature.

In the same way, if someone forgets to be polite, you do not try to act the same way. You show you are mature by being polite anyway.

Courtesy is something that gets better with practice. You must practice saying "Please" and "Thank you" (and other courteous things) if you want to always remember to say them.

ACTIVITY: List the ways your class will be more courteous. Select one to work on each week.

EXAMPLE: The class will be courteous by saying "Please" and "Thank you."

Decide how the class will monitor progress.

You may wish to put checks on the chalkboard or marbles in a jar each time the words are said.

Plan a few minutes of free time or other fun activity when a specified goal is reached.

Select some other courteous saying for the following week.

LOYALTY

OBJECTIVE: To teach the meaning of loyalty.

EXPECTATION: Students will work at developing a sense of loyalty.

DEFINITION: Faithful (firm and true) to a program, a cause, a person, an ideal or a custom.

The easiest way to teach the concept of loyalty to elementary students is to give examples of what the concept is about in an area that may be familiar to them.

EXAMPLE: Ways that a person can be loyal to his scout troop are:

He takes up for his troop.
He speaks highly of his troop. (He says good things about them.)
He supports its activities.
He verbally (with words) defends them.
He tries to make the scouts better by being a good member.

If there is a problem, he is there to help.
He does not believe "bad things" he may hear about his troop.
He does not complain about his troop.

What loyalty would it be good for a student to have?

A student should have:
Loyalty to his family.
Loyalty to his friends.
Loyalty to his school.
Loyalty to his country.
Loyalty to his beliefs about right or wrong. (Be REAL careful that religion does not enter as an issue here. This is NOT dealing with that.)

A right or wrong issue could be your belief about the dangers of gangs and drugs or your belief about the importance of studying.

To be loyal to your beliefs means, that you do not let others change your mind about things that you know are right or wrong.

Loyalty means that you do not change your beliefs in order to be liked by those who do not have the same beliefs about right and wrong that you have.

Loyalty to your family means that you believe in your family and do not want others to say unkind things about them.

Loyalty to your friends means that you say nice things about them and do not listen if someone says things that are not so good about them.

Is it ever hard to be loyal?

It is hard to be loyal when others try to change your mind.

It is hard to be loyal when others make fun of you.

It is hard to be loyal when others seem not to care.

When you are loyal to others, they will usually be loyal to you.

ACTIVITY: Divide the class into five groups. Let each group make a list of ways to be loyal.

Give each group a topic from the ones listed above.

Allow each group time to present their list to the class.

The lower grades will do better to discuss these.

With the lower grades the teacher may wish to use stuffed animals or puppets to discuss loyalty in the different areas.

CHEATING

OBJECTIVE: To establish good principles by which to live.

EXPECTATION: Students will realize personal satisfaction in earning what they achieve on their own.

DEFINITION: Cheating is a dishonest act. There are different kinds of cheating.

Cheating in a game means not to follow the rules.

Cheating on class work is using information from, another student or another source (such as a piece of paper with the answer on it) and claiming it to be your work.

Why do people cheat?

People cheat because they:
       Want to win.
       Want to look smart.
       Want to pass.

Want to get praise for a good grade.
Did not study.
Did not make an effort.
Are not good sports and can not deal with losing.

Can the students think of other reasons?

DISCUSS:

How do you feel when others cheat?

How do you feel if it seems as though the other person (or team) cheated to win?

What consequences should cheaters have?

    Suggestions:
        Put out of the game.
        Not allowed to play next time.
        Zero on a test.

Can you think of others?

Can you help students who cheat?

    Suggestions:
        Ask them to be fair.
        Tell them you do not want to play unless the game is fair.

Offer to help them study for a test.

Can you think of other ways to help?

What can you do to keep yourself from cheating?

    Suggestions:
        Study and be prepared for tests.

Take the low grade you deserve rather than cheat if you did not study.

Play the game as fairly as you want others to play with you.

Focus more on having fun than winning.

Does cheating ever work?

Sometimes, it seems to work, but only for a short time because sooner or later the person gets caught and then everyone knows he is a cheater.

If you cheat one time, you will be known as a cheater and have a bad reputation (others will think you are not honest). Then it will take a very long time before people will believe you have changed.

ACTIVITY: Discuss what happens to people caught cheating.

In the movies - what happens to people who cheat?

At games - Disqualified - Not allowed to play.
At cards - In cowboy movies - shot!
On lessons - Given a zero - Sometimes put out of college.

In real life - what happens to people who cheat?

At cards - No one wants to play with that person.
On lessons -The person receives a zero.
At games - The team gets a penalty or the whole team in put out.
On the job - The person could be fired - lose his job.

Allow the students to think of other examples of cheating and consequences.

Then spend time focusing on how to AVOID cheating.

BE YOUR BEST

OBJECTIVE: To inspire/motivate students to strive to excel.

EXPECTATION: Students will understand their own uniqueness and see a reason for striving to improve.

DEFINITION: Everyone is good at something. You can do some things better than other things.

What things do you think you do best?

Suggestions: (Students may add others.)
Read
Math
Science
Cook
Sing
Write stories
Art
Puzzles
Games
Sports

Jeanette Bradley M. Ed.

History

Which of the above do you like the least?
Which do you think is the hardest for you to do?
Are any of them easy but you do not like a great deal?

Give students time to discuss likes and dislikes.
This will probably take more than one day.
You will find that USUALLY the one you like the best is the one that you do well.

Now comes the hard part.

For things that you do NOT enjoy, you still need to try your best!

Many students say such things as:

"Math is my worst subject, that's why I make bad grades in math."
or

"My mom had trouble with math, so I'm not good at it either."

Students who say this type of thing feel that it is "O.K." to do poorly because it is their "bad subject."

That is NOT really a reason! It is a "thing" to blame, so that they do not have to admit that they are too lazy to try or would rather waste their time or play instead of study.

Likewise, students who say, "It's boring," use this as an excuse to avoid admitting that they do not want to work.

Smart students know that school work is not to entertain them, but to make them educated!

Some students who do not study think that they are not "smart" like others. When they study, they discover that they can also make good grades - maybe not all A's, but better grades than when they did not study.

If you are one who does not study some every day in school and also some at home, give it a try. You will be pleased with yourself!

Instead of using excuses for things that you do not like, work a little harder on it each day and you will get better.

Even if you do NOT enjoy something, you can get better if you try hard.

You do NOT have to try to be BETTER than others.
You do NEED to try to do YOUR BEST - whatever that is for you.

Some people who are great today in music, art, or sports were not the BEST IN THE WORLD when they started and maybe they will never be the world's best, but doing THEIR best helped them to get better and better!

Whatever your talent is try to be your best.

Whatever your weakness is, also, try to do your best in that.

There is only ONE EXACTLY like you. You are unique (even twins have SOME things different). Be yourself, but make yourself the best person that you can.

ACTIVITY: Allow the students to list excuses why some students do not try to be their best.

EXAMPLES: Others will think that I am showing off.
                 Others won't like me.
                 I don't think I'd do better.
                 I'm not smart enough to do better.
                 It's too much trouble to try.

Can you think of any more?

Jeanette Bradley M. Ed.

Why should you try to AVOID these excuses?

Have each student do the following on a piece of paper.

LIST THREE THINGS YOU WILL TRY IN ORDER TO BE YOUR BEST.

SPORTSMANSHIP

OBJECTIVE: To teach students the basic elements of good sportsmanship.

EXPECTATION: Students will be able to identify good sportsmanship conduct and work at practicing it.

DEFINITION: How a person plays or watches a game. A good sport plays for enjoyment, as well as, to win.

Things to remember about being a good sport.

A good sport:
    Tries to do his best.
    Wants to win, but ALSO plays for the fun of it.
    Plays as a team member.
    Sees that others have a turn.
    Admits that others are good at playing (even those on the other team).
    Says something nice to those who try hard.
    Says something nice to those who play well.
    Does not complain about others who miss the ball or a chance to score for the team.

Jeanette Bradley M. Ed.

Does not pout or complain if he does not get control of the ball or get to play first.

Can the students think of any other things that a good sport does?

It is easy to be a good sport when:

You are scoring points.
You have control of the ball.
Your team is winning.
Others are cheering for you.
Your team wins with a high score.

It is hard to be a good sport when:

Someone else on your team is making all the points.
Someone else has control of the ball.
You do not get a chance to have the ball.
You drop or miss the ball.
You get chosen last to be on the team.
The other team is winning.
The other team really does have bigger players.
You do not win.

When you are not winning, you need to think about the good time that you are having playing with your team.

Remember that you have the choice of being a good sport. No one makes you a poor sport - YOU CHOOSE!

You can choose to be a good sport and:

Have more friends. (People do not enjoy a poor sport.)
Enjoy the game better.
Have the reputation of being a good sport.

What can you do if you have a hard time being a good sport?

Try to spend a lot of time thinking about the FUN you have when you play.

Remember, it is better to play and lose than it is to be left out and not get to play at all.

Watch how others play and plan to try harder to do better next time.

Watch how others who are good sports act and work at doing the things that they do.

Think about the list of things that good sports do (first page of this lesson) and pick one or two at a time to work on to get better.

You can become a better sport if you really work on it. It will be HARD, but later you will be glad.

The teacher or the P. E. teacher may wish to list one or two things each week for the entire class to work on improving.
Post what the class will try to improve.
Example: Say something nice to those who try hard.

All students would try to do that by saying such such things as:

"Good try."
"Nice job."
"Way to go!"
"Great, just great."
"Terrific throw."
"Wow, look at that."

Some students have to be taught how and when to say nice things.

ACTIVITY: Let students tell about their favorite athlete.

PROMPTS: What do you like best about him? why?
                   What sport does he play?

Is he a good sport?

Do people (fans) like him?

What do most people think of poor sports?

What happens when a person makes a wrong choice in conduct during a professional game?

PROMPTS: A person who fights or disrupts the game is:

Put in the penalty box - hockey.

Sent out of the game - baseball.

Giving the other team a free throw - basketball.

Giving the other team "yards" - football.

(The player may also have to pay a big fine - especially if he caused a fight.)

Poor sportsmanship is not allowed.

You may still feel bad or upset if you do not win.

You may still hate it that you missed the ball.

You may still regret that you did not get to make points, but you do NOT have to show how you feel by such acts as:

Complaining

Shoving/ hitting/pushing

Name calling

Pouting/frowning

Yelling "Boo" or some other such words.

Try hard every time to:

Have fun.

Smile.

BE A GOOD SPORT!

SHARING

OBJECTIVE: To show that sharing is better than selfishness.

EXPECTATION: Students will begin to work on sharing.

DEFINITION: Allowing others to use your things. Shared things are returned!

What is good about sharing?

    You feel good about yourself.
    You make others happy.
    You make life more pleasant.
    When you share, others share with you.

Types of things you can share:

    Toys
    Crayons
    Story book, magazine
    Games
    Baseball cards
    A good joke
    An interesting story
    Some exciting news

Can the students add to this list?

Allow students time to discuss why these things can be shared.

Types of things that are NOT supposed to be shared.

> Your lunch. If someone does not have a lunch, let the teacher know. Your homework. Everyone needs to do their own, Your class work. Everyone needs to do their own. Money. Other students need to ask their parents (not you) if they need money.
> Personal things, such as: a purse, comb, billfold, or watch.

Can the students add to this list?

Let them discuss why these should not be shared.

When does sharing become a problem?

1. When a student believes that the item was GIVEN to him.
2. When someone wants you to share and then later they will not share with you.
3. When someone SAYS he will GIVE you something if you SHARE something (that he wants to play with) with him.

Later, when that person returns what you SHARED he wants what was GIVEN to you RETURNED.

What can be done about these problems?

First: Be REAL SURE that the other student KNOWS that you are SHARING.

Tell the other student that you are willing to SHARE, but that you will want it back.

Second: Do NOT share JUST so that others will share with you. They may not be that nice.

Share because YOU ARE a nice person. Share because you enjoy your friends. Remind the other student that you shared first and hope that he will do the same for you.

(Try not to be upset if he refuses to share.)
Do not continue to try to change the person if he refuses - FIND SOMEONE ELSE to share with.

Third: Do NOT let someone GIVE you something in order to get you to share.
Example:
"I will GIVE you this baseball card if you let me play with your football."

The other person USUALLY wants back what was GIVEN to you to let him play with your toy. After playing with your toy the other student could CLAIM that he did not give it.

Tell the other person that you will SHARE both things and when you are finished BOTH things will be returned.

Remember: You do not have to be like others.
You CHOOSE what you do.

Decide that you want to be a sharing person.

ACTIVITY: Discuss any story you have read about someone sharing or not wanting to share.

Act out the story or pantomime "sharing something" and let the class guess what you are doing.

CITIZENSHIP

OBJECTIVE: To give students an understanding of the concept of citizenship.

EXPECTATION: Every student will be able to identify the characteristics of a good citizen.

DEFINITION: The way you act as a member (a part) of the community (city/town) where you live.

EXAMPLE: If you obey school rules and show respect for others, you are good students.

If you obey government laws and show respect for people and matters of the government, you are good citizens.

A person who is a good citizen tries to:

Obey all the rules - even when no one is watching.
Respect the rights and property of others.
Be helpful when someone has a need.
Show respect for public officials.

Show respect for the flag.
Show pride in his country.
Show loyalty to his country.

Can students think of other things that a good citizen does?

A good citizen does not always agree with government rules or with people in the government, but he obeys the rules and respects the people because a good citizen knows that the government tries to do what is best for all people.

When is it hard to be a good citizen?

1. When no one is watching what you do.

    Example: You would not damage benches or flowers in the park if there were a policeman nearby.
    But, would you be just as good if no one were watching you?

2. When you hear others say bad things about or to government officials.

    Example: Sometimes on T. V. people say rude (VERY ugly) things about the government or government officials. They usually do it to get people to laugh.
    (There is a difference between funny and VERY RUDE things.)
    You may think is sounds good and go around making fun of the person. The person you would be making fun of may really be trying to do his best.

If you really disagree with something he did, the proper thing to do is to write a polite letter to the government person and tell about your concerns and how you think it could be made better.

3.   When you do not feel like following rules.

Examples   When you feel like it, following rules is easy. But to have to do it every, every day gets hard.

When you follow rules and show respect for people and matters of the government you are a good citizen.

Remember: You show respect when you act in a special polite manner.

Students sometimes have more trouble showing respect for government property than for government officials.

Example: Some students like to pick or pull up flowers in public places. Some students like to climb on monuments and/or statues and sometimes cause damage.

These things seem like fun things to do, but remember, being a good citizen means not to damage things.

ACTIVITY: Make a wall mural of the school neighborhood.

Let the students do the drawing or collecting of pictures for it.

Suggestions for the mural:
    Buildings
    Children on the sidewalks respecting property, especially flowers.

A flag being raised - near the school or another government building.
(Many students do not realize that public schools are government property.)
A policeman talking to students.
Students and parents (in cars) obeying traffic signs.
People putting trash in containers instead of on the ground.

Let students think of other ideas and add them to the mural.

Display the mural in the class or the hallway.

Invite a policeman or persons from city hall to speak to the students about good citizenship.

MANNERS

OBJECTIVE: To show students that manners make life more pleasant.

EXPECTATION: Students will work to improve their manners.

DEFINITION: A way of acting. A rule of social conduct that is aimed at making life pleasant.

There are manners that are used at different times. Some are used at home, some at school, and some are used in certain places or buildings.

The following manners should be listed under the appropriate category.

Some may be listed in more than one place. Allow the students to help decide where to put each type of manner.

Write the following on a chart, overhead projector, chalkboard or large tablet.

HOME   SCHOOL   PUBLIC BUILDING
                              Library or Hospital

Decide under which of these should the following manners be listed.

Things that you do that are considered "manners."

In regard to speaking:

> Speak softly.
> Speak politely.
> Do not speak with your mouth full.
> Say "Please," "Thank you," and "Excuse me, please."
> Greet people - "Hi," or "Good morning."
>
> Do not make rude noises with your mouth.
> Do not raise your voice.
> Do not use rude gestures or rude "body language" when you speak.
>
> Do not "mumble." Speak clearly so that others can understand you easily.
> If you do not understand the other person, ask POLITELY for the person to repeat what was said. Avoid saying such things as, "Huh?" "What?" "What's that?" Instead try: "Will you please repeat that."

In regard to others speaking:

> Give others a chance to speak - Do not "hog" the conversation.
> Listen quietly when others are speaking.
> Do not interrupt.
> Say nice things such as, "I hope you are better soon." or "It is so nice to see you."

When a mistake is made:

> Apologize when you do or say something you should not have.

Accept another person's apology when one is offered. Say something such as, "I accept your apology," or "That is alright."

When going from one place to another:

Do not walk between two people who are speaking to each other.
Walk quietly.
Do not run.
Wait your turn. Do not rush to get ahead of others.
Do not walk to the front of the line and expect a "cut" in line.

In other areas:

If you drop something pick it up.
Return things that you borrow.
Do not put your elbows on the table as you eat.
Do not stuff your mouth when you eat.
Laugh at funny things, but NOT at people.
Apologize if you bump into someone.

Can the students think of others?

People often judge what type of person you are by your manners.

Manners are ONE sign of being mature (grown up - for your age).

Think about how many of the above you already knew.

How many do you do every day?

Which could you work on to have better manners?

These are different for each student. Decide what manners you need to improve or let your teacher help.

ACTIVITY: Challenge another class to see who can be the best mannered.

Ask other faculty members to observe both classes and decide who wins.

The librarian, the nurse, the principal, or the P. E. and music teachers would be good judges.

SELF - IMAGE

OBJECTIVE: To assist student development (or increase) of a positive self - image and to identify personal strengths, weaknesses, and uniqueness.

EXPECTATION: Students will have an increased self-understanding or his abilities, interest, personality, and achievement.

DEFINITION: What you think of yourself or your opinion of how good you are.

When you think about how wonderful you are, you need to think of how you "see" yourself.

What do you think you are like?

The character traits - the way you act, your talents, and interest and hobbies make up the part of you that others see and that affects how they feel about you.

Those things can be stated as:

Personality   Talent/Abilities   Hobbies/Interest

When you understand what types of things are in these areas you will be able to "see" yourself better.

Personality is the way you act toward yourself and others.

Talent/Ability is skill in one or more areas that you do well.

Hobbies/Interest are the things that you enjoy and try to find time to do them. (Usually done in what is considered "spare time.")

Have the class name things that are considered personality traits.

Personality traits include (but are not limited to):

Friendly	Kind
Thoughtful	Talkative
Caring	Lazy
Honest	Selfish
Shy	Generous
Helpful	Temperamental
Sincere	Cheerful
Positive	Complainer
Fair	Responsible
Dependable	Loyal
Good Sport	Courteous

Can the students think of others that they want to add?

Pick out four or five that you are MOST of the time.

Pick out two or three that you WANT to be.

Talent/Abilities: What are you best at doing?

Reading	Math	Science
Sports	Singing	Musical Instrument

Drawing	Swimming	Cooking
Organized	Sewing	Building Things
Writing	Games	Telling Stories
Memory	Skating	Making Friends
Fishing	Dancing	Gymnastics

Can the students add to the list?

Think of the ones that you do best.
It does NOT mean which you do better than other people.
It does mean it is what YOU do best!

Your hobby or main interest may be the same as your talent.

Example:

> If you are really good at skating that is a talent and you probably spent all the time that you can skating, so, it can also be your hobby.

Hobbies/Interest: What do you enjoy spending your time doing?

Sports	Clubs/Scouts	Reading
Pen Pal	Drawing	Coin Collection
Pets	Bicycling	Music
Cooking	Hiking	Camping

Can the students add more?

IMPORTANT FACT:

> No one is perfect!

> Everyone is good at some things.

> Everyone is better at some things than at others.

You can be GOOD at something WITHOUT being a "winner" or the best in the class at it.

You can enjoy what you are good at WITHOUT worrying what others do.

If you like yourself, you will use your best character traits so that others will like you also.

If you found some personality trait in yourself that you do not like, you can work at getting rid of it.

EXAMPLE: If you are lazy, you can begin to work harder.

ACTIVITY: Make a display using one of the following.

                   Let students draw their pictures or use school pictures.

Suggested titles:

WE SHINE LIKE STARS!
Mount the pictures on stars.

OR

A GREAT BUNCH OF STUDENTS

Mount the pictures on "grapes."

OR

Do a class TALENT CHAIN.

Mount or draw class (or put names) on chain (like "charm bracelet").

On any of the above list a talent, hobby or good trait of each student.

FINALLY:

Let students list all the reasons to feel good about themselves.

EXAMPLE: I am wonderful because I am:

Smart in _____.

Talented in _____.

Having fun with my hobby of

_____

Everyone is special and unique! Enjoy being YOU!

THOUGHTFULNESS

OBJECTIVE: To make students aware of how nice it is to be thoughtful.

EXPECTATION: Students will practice being thoughtful of others.

DEFINITION: Thoughtfulness is thinking about others and doing something for them without being asked or told to do so.

EXAMPLES: You are thoughtful if you help your mother before she tells you to help.
You are thoughtful if you help a new student make friends without being told.
You are thoughtful if you help a person pick up things that he dropped without being asked.

You are thoughtful (and mannerly) if you hold the door open for another person to pass.

> You are thoughtful if you ask about the welfare of others.
> "How is your brother who was sick?"

Thoughtful people try to help others:

> Even when they are not asked.
> Even if they will not get anything for doing it.
> Even when they do not like what has to be done.
> Without fussing about helping.

Thoughtful people are doing things because they like to help others.

They like people and want to help make life better for others even if it is just in little ways.

Thoughtful people are liked and appreciated by others because:

> They are helpful.
> They are glad to help and that lets us know we can count on them.
> Their thoughtfulness makes us feel liked.
> Their thoughtfulness makes life more pleasant.

Has the class read any story that had someone who was thoughtful?

Does any student know of a book that he read that has a thoughtful person?

Do the students know any real person that is a very thoughtful person.

Discuss exactly what happened in the stories or in real life that made the students think that the person was thoughtful.

Can the students think of other ways to be thoughtful that have not been mentioned?

When are times that you like for others to be thoughtful to you?

PROMPTS: When you feel bad.
                  When you have had a hard day.
                  When you have to start at a new school.
                  When you move to a new neighborhood.

Remember: Thoughtful people are not doing things to get
                  something in return.

ACTIVITY: On the chalkboard or a chart write:

A THOUGHTFUL DAY

BEFORE SCHOOL   DURING SCHOOL   AFTER SCHOOL

Under the headings list thoughtful acts that can be done and later put
a check by any that the students did during the day. (The After School
list will need to be checked the following day.)

The day should be very pleasant!

CHEERFULNESS/HAPPINESS

OBJECTIVE: To teach students that cheerfulness and happiness are choices.

EXPECTATION: Students will understand that they can choose to be happy or not in most situations.

DEFINITION: Full of gladness, enjoyment, and well-being.

EXAMPLES: You are happy when you visit friends. You are happy when your parents are pleased with you. You are cheerful when you feel good. You are cheerful when you get your way.

FACTS ABOUT HAPPINESS:

Things can get you excited (such as a new toy), but they do not give you lasting happiness.

People can make you excited and happy because their love and friendship can be lasting.

You can be happy and cheerful if you are poor or if you are rich. What you have does not make you happy. How you CHOOSE to feel makes you happy.

You can have a lot of things and not be happy because you think about what you do not have. You can have a little and be happy with that.

Even people who are sick and do not spend all of the time complaining are considered cheerful.

You live in the greatest country. You are getting a good education. You have a place to live. These are all reasons to be happy.

If you spend time helping others, you will feel happy with yourself.

Happiness needs to be shared.

Think about the good things that you do have.

What do you have that can help you be happy?
    Family?
    Place to live?
    Health?
    Food?
    Talents?
    Friends?

Can you think of others?

The opposite, of course, is sadness.

You are sad when you are lonely, troubled, and have serious problems such as illness or death, or maybe even divorce in your family.

These are part of life and you live with it and accept the fact that this is the time that you need to be close to your friends and family.

You can still feel happy that you have their support and care.

You can also remember that you are NOT always faced with really serious problems.

There are many children who are physically handicapped and they lead very cheerful lives.

They do not focus on what they can not do.
They work on enjoying what they can do.

So happiness and cheerfulness really are CHOICES, because they are how you CHOOSE to be.

You can choose every day to enjoy life.

ACTIVITY: Have students make two circles - one inside the other.

They need to be in pairs facing each other.

If there is an odd number, the teacher will need to participate.

The students on the inside circle tell something that happened to them to make them feel happy.

Then everyone moves to the next person to their right.

This time the students on the outside tells something that has made them feel cheerful.

This can continue for one turn or more so that each student gets a chance to talk.

Encourage students to enjoy life by CHOOSING to be happy and cheerful.

DRUG FREE

OBJECTIVE: To teach students why drugs are not good for them.

EXPECTATION: Students will know some facts about the dangers of drugs and some techniques for saying no to drugs.

DEFINITION: A substance used in medicine or a narcotic that has some effect on the body.

MEDICINE: Medicine is a drug that is used under certain conditions to relieve pain or help the body heal.

Medicine should only be used as prescribed on the label or under the supervision of a doctor.

It is not safe for one person to use medicine prescribed by a doctor for someone else - even if the symptoms SEEM to be exactly the same.

Some medicine can be habit forming (Your body starts depending on it.) and should be used with caution.

DRUGS/NARCOTICS These drugs also cause changes in the body.
They can kill you.

Drugs are habit forming, (You can not get along without them.)

Drugs can cause uncontrollable behavior in you.

Drugs are against the law.

Some drugs can change your body so badly that the doctors can not get you completely well.

Drugs can make you feel good for a while, but when they wear off, they make you feel real sick.

If drugs are so bad, why do students (and others, even adults) use them?

Some students use drugs because:

 They want to know what it is like.
 They want to feel "cool."
 They do not want to seem "chicken."

 They think it makes them have fun.

 They want to be part of the group.
 They do not feel good about themselves.
 They think they are "grown up" doing it.
 They believe others who tell them that it is O.K. to do drugs.

Ways to avoid drugs:

Make YOUR OWN CHOICES!

Do not follow others - who do drugs.

Do not let others tease or threaten you into starting or trying drugs.

Feel good about who you are and what talents you have. Students who are pleased with themselves know that they do not need drugs.

Have a hobby or be involved in fun things, so that you do not use drugs for "something to do."

Spend time with good friends - CHOOSE your friends carefully.

How to say no to drugs:

SOUND SURE OF YOURSELF.
"No, I don't want any.

BE FIRM. Do not act like you might change your mind.
"No, thank you."

ANSWER CLEARLY so that they will not misunderstand your answer.

"No, it is not good for me."

ALSO TRY - Ignore them, do not listen to them.

Refusing drugs is one of the most important things that you can do for yourself!

ACTIVITY:

Many students enjoy writing skits on refusing drugs - the good guys telling the bad guys no.

This is a good time to let them share with another class. They could put on their skits.

Students also enjoy acting out just the "saying no" part. Give them the opportunity. They can be very creative.

This will probably be a good place to STRESS not talking to strangers.

Students need to be told never to talk to strangers and to refuse to accept anything that may be offered.

DON'T TALK! RUN!

If they are approached by strangers with drugs or otherwise, they need to be told to be sure to report it to parents and/or teachers.

Since drugs are a serious topic and one that so many students come into contact with (now or later), a great deal of time needs to be spent on stressing the dangers of drugs and how to avoid them.

POSITIVE THINKING

POSITIVE THINKING

OBJECTIVE: To promote a positive outlook on life in order for the student to be happier.

EXPECTATION: Students will learn skills on how to be happier.

DEFINITION: Think about the good part of whatever you have or whatever you are doing.

Some of the time you do not realize how well off you are.

List some of the good things that you have that many children do not have.

EXAMPLES: A good family
Friends
Food every day
A chance for a good education
Medicine when you are ill
A place to live
Air-conditioning and heating
T.V., Bike, Skateboard, etc.

Many children in the world (even in the U.S.) do not have many of these.

Since you are so lucky, you need to try to think how you can enjoy what you have.

Also, any time that you can, try to make it even better.

Sometimes, things happen that you do not like.
Things will go wrong even when you try hard.

But do not make a bad thing worse by complaining CONSTANTLY. Everyone probably complains SOME. It is the CONSTANT complaining that others find hard to listen to.

Are there any ways that things that you do not like can be made better?

First, remember that you can not change everything to please you.

Second, if you can not change a situation that you do not like, try some of the following to make it easier for you.

> Do not exaggerate about how things are.
> (Many people like to exaggerate how bad things are so others will feel sorry for them).
>
> Smile! Smile! It makes you FEEL better.
>
> Be GLAD that things are not worse.
>
> If you made a wrong choice, learn from you mistake and try to do better.
>
> When you visit friends, talk about happy things.
>
> If you feel you are being "picked on," tell the teacher. Maybe you are not. Or maybe you are causing part of your problem. You will feel better if you get help from the teacher.
>
> Try to see the happy side of things. Look for good things.

Good is there, you just have to notice it.

If you feel that you were corrected and you were not guilty, remember ALL the times that you DID do something and the teacher did not see you. (And you did not report yourself - You "got away" with it!) This time "evens up" those times.

Happy people do not always have happy things happen to them.

They CHOOSE to be happy.

Begin being happy with positive thinking.

Focus on (think about) the GOOD things in life! Sometimes you can only find PART of a situation that can help you with happy thoughts, but PRACTICE LOOKING for those good parts!

Allow students to discuss these concepts.

ACTIVITY: Draw things (or use pictures) such as:
                   candy
                   lemon
                   donut
                   books
                   rain (drops)
                   school house
                   pet
                   money
                   T.V.

Students may add to the list.
Have the students list (or discuss) what is good and what can be a problem with each of them.

EXAMPLE: You can be happy with a donut or upset that it has a hole in it. Lemons are really sour, but they are great in a pie.

Lesson to learn - You can be happy if you THINK about the POSITIVE parts of things in life.
Try - it may take practice.

NEW STUDENTS

OBJECTIVE: To teach students how to accept others.

EXPECTATION: Students will gain skills in accepting new students.

DEFINITION: A boy or girl that moves to your neighborhood.

When you see new students come to our class you are excited.

You want to know about the new students.

Who are they?

Where did they come from?

What are they like?

Will they be friendly?

Will they be smart?

You want to know all of these things, but what you need to be thinking about first is how do the new students feel?

Also, what are some things that the new students will want to know about you?

New students are usually nervous.

Why?

Would you be nervous?

Have you ever been the new student at a school?

What are some reasons why new students may be nervous?

PROMPTS:	They may be sad about leaving their other schools.
	They do not know anyone here.
	They do not know where to go to find places that they may need. (Restroom. library, etc.)
	They do not know if you will be friendly to them (or how long it will take them to make new friends).
	They do not know the school rules and worry that they may break a rule that they do not know about.
	They do not know what the teacher expects.

How can you help?

Smile! That will let them know that you are friendly.

At lunch time or free time talk to the new students.

Tell the new students something good about your class so they will be glad to be a part of it.

Ask about them. Where are they from?

Show that you are glad to have new students in your class.

Tell them something good about the teacher.

Help introduce them to others.

ACTIVITY: Let the class plan and practice carrying out some of the above conversations to be used when new students arrive.

                        Let the students who have been "new students" tell what it was like.

                        Plan a "Buddy" system that could help new students. The class will take turns being the "Buddy."
A "Buddy" is a helper to new students.

VI.

DISCIPLINE CHARTS

VI. DISCIPLINE CHARTS

Suggestions:

1. Make a chart showing grading system.
   Example: 1 - 2 checks = A
                   3 - 4 checks = B
                   5 - 6 checks = C etc.

   Post list of students' names near or on grading system chart.
   Put checks by student's name for each offense.

   Add consequences (Such as) at bottom of chart.
   1 - 2   checks REMINDER
   3   checks WARNING
   4   checks CALL PARENT
   5   checks ISOLATION
   6   checks CONFERENCE WITH
             PRINCIPAL
          etc.

2. Use poster with library pocket cards glued on (or some other means of posting pocket cards). Recommended for grades PreK - 2.

   One pocket with each student's name on it
   Cut colored strips of paper:
   Green - Good
   Yellow - Warning
   Purple - Call or note to parent
   Red - Consequence (According to rule broken).

   With strips of paper in pocket cards in the above order, tell students they will move front (top) color (green) to the back of pocket as disruptions occur. Colors will be moved for each offense.

Start each week with green. Green could be equal to A in conduct, etc.

At any given time, students can see their grades.

3. Individual conduct card.
   Recommended for grades 3 - 5.
   Conduct marks are marked on one side for offenses and ink stamps or teacher initials on the other side for good deeds.

   A set number of good marks could cancel a bad grade.

   Example: TEN good marks could cancel ONE bad mark.
   They really work hard to cancel out marks and this produces good conduct.

   The number of bad marks determines the grade for the week.
   A new card is used each week.
   The number of bad marks ALSO determines consequences.

Each grade level should determine the number of marks for each conduct grade.

Class rules:

Parents should be notified of the class rules at the beginning of the year (Best if they sign a copy).

(Parents also need to be notified of the program at a conference, meeting or news letter.)

Different schools select different methods.

Whatever record keeping system is used, consideration should be given to rewarding good effort not just noticing the negative.

While discipline cards and grades are useful they are NOT the main means of changing behavior in a lasting positive manner.

Sample conduct card (Copies for students can be run on light tagboard.)

RULE # 1	Rule # 2	Rule # 3	Rule # 4	Rule # 5
Follow directions the first time they are given.	If I recognize your voice you will receive a consequence.	Stay in your seat unless given permission to get up.	No teasing name calling, or sign of disrespect.	Raise your hand and wait to be recognized to speak.

Name   Date

P.E.   Restroom   Library   Music   Art   Hall   Lunch   Outside

Sample class rules:

Be courteous to everyone.
Allow body "space."
Keep hands and feet to self.
Follow directions.
Avoid disrupting class.

Or

Raise your hand to be recognized to speak.
Follow directions.
Do not name call or fight.
Stay in your desk.
Do not talk without permission.

The teacher and the students need to decide what they want.

Remember: It is not the type of discipline card or rules that will determine success.

Success will be measured by the degree that you TEACH students how to make Right Choices and accept RESPONSIBILITY for their CHOICES.

VII.

COUPONS

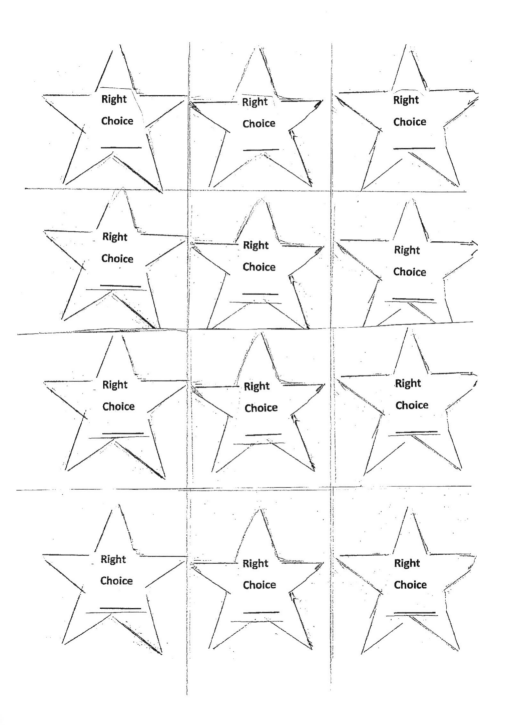

VIII.

CERTIFICATES

Right Choice
Award
for good choices

Presented to

_____

Year _____ Grade _____

RIGHT CHOICE
Improvement
Award

Presented to

_____

for

_____

Year _____ Grade _____

Printed in the United States
By Bookmasters